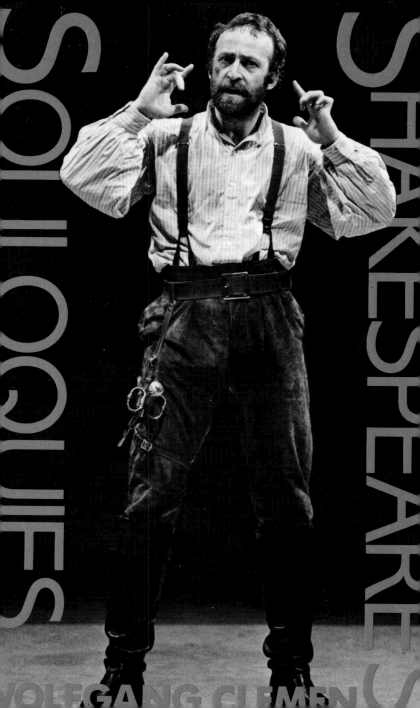

Shakespeare's Soliloquies

Shakespeare's Soliloquies

WOLFGANG CLEMEN

Translated by
Charity Scott Stokes

METHUEN & CO. LTD
LONDON AND NEW YORK

First published in 1987 by
Methuen & Co. Ltd
11 New Fetter Lane, London EC4P 4EE

Published in the USA by
Methuen & Co.
in association with Methuen, Inc.
29 West 35th Street, New York, NY 10001

Typeset in Monophoto Baskerville by
Vision Typesetting, Manchester
Printed in Great Britain by Richard Clay Ltd,
Bungay, Suffolk

British Library Cataloguing in Publication Data
Clemen, Wolfgang
Shakespeare's soliloquies.
1. Shakespeare, William—Criticism and interpretation
2. Soliloquy
I. Title II. Shakespeares monologe. *Eine zugang zu seiner dramatischen
Kunst.*
822.3′3   PR2997.S7

ISBN 0-416-05862-0
ISBN 0-416-30460-5 Pbk

Library of Congress Cataloguing in Publication Data
Clemen, Wolfgang.
Shakespeare's soliloquies.

Translation of: Shakespeares Monologe.
Bibliography: p.
1. Shakespeare, William, 1564–1616—Technique.
2. Soliloquy.   I. Title.
PR2997.S7C5   1987   822.3′3   87–1541

ISBN 0-416-05862-0
ISBN 0-416-30460-5 (pbk.)

Contents

Preface   ix

1 INTRODUCTION   1

2 SOLILOQUIES FROM THE HISTORY
   PLAYS   13

   RICHARD III
   Enter Richard, Duke of Gloucester, solus
   (I.i.1–41)   15
   Richard awakes from his nightmare – his last
   soliloquy (V.iii.178–207)   19

   RICHARD II
   Richard II's prison soliloquy (V.v.1–66)   23

   KING JOHN
   The Bastard as commentator   29
   His speech on commodity (II.i.561–98)   30

   HENRY IV, PART TWO
   Sleeplessness – the lot of kingship (III.i.1–31)   32
   Prince Hal on the glory and burden of the crown
   (IV.v.19–46)
                                                                                            35
   HENRY IV, PART ONE
   Falstaff's reflections on honour (V.i.125–41)   38

3 SOLILOQUIES FROM THE COMEDIES AND ROMANCES   45

TWO GENTLEMEN OF VERONA
Launce and his dog (II.iii.1–32)   46

TWELFTH NIGHT
Malvolio's appearance in the garden scene, with eavesdroppers (II.v.143–79)   51

ALL'S WELL THAT ENDS WELL
Helena reveals her hidden love (I.i.75–96, 212–25)   60

MEASURE FOR MEASURE
Angelo discovers his human nature (II.ii.162–87)   65

CYMBELINE
Iachimo in Imogen's bedchamber (II.ii.11–51)   72

THE TEMPEST
Prospero renounces his magic power (V.i.33–57)   79

4 SOLILOQUIES FROM THE TRAGEDIES   89

ROMEO AND JULIET
Romeo's nocturnal soliloquy in the orchard (II.ii.1–25)   91
Juliet longs for her wedding night (III.ii.1–31)   95
Juliet resolves to drink the potion (IV.iii.12–58)   100
Romeo enters the tomb (V.iii.72–120)   104

JULIUS CAESAR
Brutus torn by inner conflict (II.i.1–85)   109

HAMLET
Hamlet's soliloquies: introductory survey   119
Hamlet's rejection of the world (I.ii.129–59)   126
Hamlet's 'To be, or not to be' (III.i.56–90)   132

MACBETH

Lady Macbeth reads her husband's letter
(I.v.1–30)
                             141
Her pact with the infernal powers (I.v.38–54)   142
Macbeth shrinks back from the murder
(I.vii.1–28)
                             149
Macbeth's dagger soliloquy (II.i.31–64)   156

OTHELLO

Othello's final soliloquy (V.ii.1–22)   163

KING LEAR

Lear's soliloquizing speeches   171
Lear's visions (IV.vi.151–75)   173

5 CONCLUSION   179

NOTES   193
SELECT BIBLIOGRAPHY   210

Preface

This little book, which was originally published in German, is conceived as an introduction to Shakespeare's soliloquies in all their complexity. By presenting a selection of some twenty-odd passages, followed by detailed commentary, it tries to convey an idea of Shakespeare's stagecraft, his exceptional theatrical judgement and his evocative use of poetic language. The extracts cover all periods and genres of his work but, due to its confined scope, this study obviously cannot claim to be anything like a systematic and comprehensive presentation of all the important types of soliloquy in Shakespeare's drama. This book is intended not only for the student of Renaissance drama but also for theatre practitioners and for the general reader. It aims to provide some insight into individual aspects of Shakespeare's verbal and dramatic art as well as offering some suggestions for further ways of looking at the themes, motifs and characterization of the plays under discussion.

No attempt has been made, however, to incorporate a critical discussion of the vast secondary literature on each play, although the notes do refer the reader to a selection of relevant publications. As this study is meant to be an introduction and also seeks to meet the needs of the general

reader, considerations of a more theoretical or meth-
odological nature have been kept to a minimum.

References to Shakespeare's texts throughout are to the
Arden editions of individual plays. Details of those Arden
editions from which the selected soliloquy passages have
been taken are given in full in the bibliography at the end.

For this English version Dr Ingeborg Boltz contributed
not only most of the notes (which had to be adapted for an
English reading public) and the references to stage history,
but also numerous substantial additions and necessary
changes to the original German text. I wish to express my
warmest thanks for her competent and very constructive
assistance. Many thanks are also due to Dr Charity Scott
Stokes for coping with difficult problems of translation.

1

Introduction

When we have been reading a Shakespeare play, or have seen one in the theatre, we may feel the need to attain a closer and more precise understanding of it. We sense that this can happen only through the study of individual aspects of the plays. Although it is by Shakespeare as a whole that we are affected, yet this whole can only be approached by the study of individual elements – by a scene, a passage, a certain manner of representation or a recurring element of the drama.

The soliloquies, some of which have been selected for examination in this volume, are one of the elements through which we may gain access to the whole. Their study is particularly fruitful in enabling us to grasp something of the distinctive quality of Shakespeare's craftsmanship, being in-miniature reflections of his art of language and characterization, and his skill of dovetailing in the construction of scenes. Each soliloquy is connected in different ways and at different levels with the dramatic organism as a whole. There are more than 300 soliloquies in Shakespeare's plays and we find them in every play, but their frequency in the individual plays varies, as does their length, which ranges from half a line to seventy. Yet this is less remarkable than the extraordinary variety of their design and function, reflecting the diversity of Shakespeare's plays as a whole. This is most apparent when a comparison is made between Shakespeare's soliloquies and those of other great dramatists, such as Calderón or Racine, Lessing or Schiller. Each of these writers developed his own distinctive types of soliloquy, yet in each case the soliloquies remained within certain limits. Thus it is possible to speak of the typical soliloquy as found in Racine or Schiller, or of the soliloquy typical of Senecan tragedy. We would find ourselves in a predicament if we wanted to speak in the same way of the typical soliloquy in Shakespeare, for there are not only the great reflections of the tragic heroes, Hamlet's 'To be or not to be' (III.i) and Macbeth's 'If it were done, when 'tis done' (I.vii), but also the comic one-man scene mounted by Launce in *Two Gentlemen of Verona* (II.iii) with his shoes and his dog; the catechism with which Falstaff dissects the concept of honour (*1 Henry IV*, V.i); the reaction of Malvolio to the forged letter (*Twelfth Night*, II.v), in which the comic effect is enhanced still further by the eavesdropping; Lear's challenge to the tempestuous forces of nature (III.ii); and Prospero's summoning of the elves and spirits prior to his renunciation of magic (V.i). All these soliloquies are typical of Shakespeare, and yet they differ from one another to such a degree that no definition, however wide its terms of reference, could encompass what they have in common. Not only do they differ in style and structure, they also serve quite different purposes. Even if we were to postulate several basic types of soliloquy in Shakespeare, following the functional patterns found in drama before his time – as has already been done[1] – we would only partially succeed in assigning to them the abundance of individual soliloquies. For all such categories as expositional soliloquy, self-characterizing soliloquy, reflective soliloquy, homily and so on, turn out to be applicable in part only. They can be better applied to the shorter, less remarkable soliloquies, which tend to follow the scheme of traditional convention more closely. What we think of as Shakespeare's great soliloquies can hardly be classified in this way, for in them, if we do look for these basic types, we find several at a time, interrelated, and the decisive factor is in any case not the type, or pattern, but what transcends it.

Nevertheless, when Shakespeare began to write his plays he found soliloquies as part of the established tradition[2]. In this area, as elsewhere, it becomes evident that Shakespeare's creative genius was not only in innovation, but that he was also an inspired borrower who took whatever he required from heterogeneous sources, in order to develop it further into new combinations.

Elizabethan drama was founded on the conjunction of the most diverse dramatic genres and styles. Mystery play and morality play, Senecan tragedy and euphuistic comedy, popular spectacle, pageant and masque – all these had given rise to a theatre which accommodated allegorical representation and realism, the use of rhetoric and colloquial speech. Dramatists employed the full range of so-called conventions in order to inform and instruct the spectators, to appeal to their power of imagination, but also to remind them of the fictionality of their theatrical experience, varying the manner of presentation from the most direct to the most indirect.[3] The development of the soliloquy up to the time immediately preceding Shakespeare already reflects the diversity of this expansive dramatic tradition.

Today we tend to associate the soliloquy primarily with meditation and the expression of emotion, with introspection and with what Matthew Arnold called 'the dialogue of the mind with itself'.[4] Most of the reference works also provide us with a definition of this sort, tracing it back to St Augustine, who is said to have coined the word *soliloquium*. Yet in pre-Shakespearean drama it was only occasionally used for purposes which had to do with reflection or inner conflict; more often it fulfilled the function of chorus, of 'suprapersonal' utterance, of exhortation, of clarification of the plot, above all of exposition, looking both backwards and forwards, as the prologue and the chorus had often done. In a soliloquy a character could make himself and his plans known; at times he could also give an account of events off-stage, or introduce a character who was not to appear on stage until later. Frequently dramatists used the soliloquy for epic, narrative and descriptive purposes, that is to say for material which could not easily be fitted into the play in any other way. Soliloquies could also provide a running commentary on the intricacies of the plot, and be a means of linking one scene with another, facilitating the audience's grasp of what was happening. Often the address to the audience might seem to be nothing more than a stopgap, bridging the time between exits and entrances when the stage might otherwise have remained empty.[5] It is clear that all this could not contribute to the dramatic effectiveness of the soliloquy. Time and again one recognizes the striving for clarification which characterized the mode of presentation and the style and language of the pre-Shakespearean drama, and which can still be discerned in Shakespeare's early plays.

The soliloquy of pre-Shakespearean drama was regularly addressed directly to the audience, forging a link between them and the stage. With the same nonchalance as is displayed by the biblical mystery plays of the Middle Ages and, indeed, by popular drama of all eras, the actors speak to the audience repeatedly during the play and take them into their confidence, making them privy to the entanglements which are to follow.

This direct address of the audience is important for the understanding of Shakespeare's soliloquies. The open stage protruding right into the pit, with the audience on three sides, favoured close contact, even intimacy, and a secret understanding between the audience and the soliloquizing actor[6] who was able to project his emotions by means of gestures, physiognomy and stage business. To quote J.R. Brown: 'the actors did not address the audience as if it were in another world. There was a reciprocal relationship; the audience could participate in the drama as easily as the actors could share a joke or enlist sympathy'.[7]

This stage practice is often taken into consideration in modern Shakespeare productions, although the great soliloquies have sometimes been performed quite differently, in such a way as to suggest that the actor is talking to himself alone, oblivious of everything around him.[8] In this connection it is worth noting that John Barton, one of the Royal Shakespeare Company's leading producers, when asked whether such a speech should be spoken to oneself or shared with the audience, gave the answer: 'I personally believe that it's right ninety-nine times out of a hundred to share a soliloquy with the audience.'[9]

Words that were addressed to an Elizabethan audience in this way were felt to be true, to have a higher degree of objective validity than speeches exchanged between characters. Thus the soliloquy has with some justification been said to have contributed to the force of conviction, to the veracity and credibility of the Elizabethan theatre. However, with Shakespeare another question becomes relevant, namely, to what extent does a soliloquy now also give expression to a false or distorted self-image, to an element of self-deception, or even a deliberate attempt to deceive others? This has been discussed time and again in Shakespeare criticism.

To what extent are the conventions and functions associated with the soliloquy, as outlined in the preceding paragraphs, continued in Shakespeare? What is there in the soliloquies that can be traced back to earlier dramatic tradition, and what is there that is different? The following chapters will offer some suggestions on that score, although our study is not primarily devoted to historical or comparative investigations. In brief – and therefore without sufficient differentiation – it may be said that several functions which had previously been fulfilled by the soliloquy, have in Shakespeare been ingeniously assigned to the dialogue, and tend to merge less obtrusively with other elements of dramatic representation. The epic and narrative passages which often dominated the pre-Shakespearean soliloquies may thus appear less obtrusive and may be fitted into the appropriate dramatic situation. Material of an informative or instructive kind, or general observations, which were communicated very directly in pre-Shakespearean soliloquies, are subtly interwoven into successive scenes in Shakespeare's plays. Instead of being static interruptions or 'insets' – comparable to the set speeches of Senecan tragedy[10] – Shakespeare's soliloquies became an organic part of his dramatic compositions, and this process began early on. It becomes apparent also that the instinctive dramatist in Shakespeare sensed early on the latent possibilities of dramatization within the soliloquy, of the process whereby monologue becomes dialogue, the speaker being split into selves which are in conflict with one another. Much of what distinguishes Shakespeare's soliloquies from those of his predecessors may be attributed to this process of dramatization, a skill which he developed gradually. The effectiveness of this technique is enhanced by what T.S. Eliot has called 'the attitude of self-dramatization assumed by some of Shakespeare's heroes'[11], for several of Shakespeare's characters are of an extrovert, histrionic disposition, and enjoy speaking of themselves as of another self.

Another phenomenon is revealed to us in gradual stages: Shakespeare increasingly discovers the aptness of the soliloquy as a mode of human expression, treating it as a necessary supplement to dialogue, not just as a useful, or even indispensable, dramaturgical device. Thus in Shakespeare we note these two concurrent skills: with great ease he makes such use of the traditional conventions as may suit his purposes, and with equal freedom he exceeds the bounds of these conventions, achieving new and original creative techniques which bear witness to an unprecedented understanding of human nature.

What is meant by 'convention' in this context? It means an agreement between an author and his public, an understanding that certain modes of presentation, intended to achieve certain effects, will be accepted. Convention can involve a process of simplification or abbreviation. It may enable the author to enrich the drama with perspectives and elements which could not have been included if adherence to the laws operating in real life had been demanded. Drama in itself, unfolding on the stage in front of us, presupposes our willingness to let ourselves be captivated by the fiction, and thus represents a convention. The bridging and the compression of time, the change of place, the disguises – these are only some of the dramatic conventions which we accept without hesitation.

One could, however, distinguish between permanent conventions of this nature, which have always been part of drama, and such conventions as may well be described as temporary[12], such as the use of verse, the personification of abstract qualities, or the inclusion of supernatural events and figures. For many centuries one of the conventions accepted without question was that characters on the stage should think aloud and talk to themselves, while such behaviour was regarded as a pathological deviation from the norm in real life. However, under the influence of neo-classicism and awakening rationalism, objections were raised to this stage practice, demanding that thinking aloud should be restricted to short exclamations at most. As early as 1717 the Earl of Mulgrave wrote in his 'Essay on Poetry':

> First then, Soliloquies had need be few,
> Extremely short, and spoke in passion too.[13]

Criticism, particularly of lengthy soliloquies, became more severe towards the end of the nineteenth century. Dramatists tried to make do without this convention altogether, or tried at least to motivate it realistically, as the expression of a disturbed mind, or as the largely unconscious words of a character half asleep or intoxicated. Thus the drama critic William Archer (1852–1924), who won fame through his translation of Ibsen's plays, was of the opinion that 'a few broken exclamations under high emotion is all the soliloquy that strict art should permit, for high emotion does in many cases manifest itself in speech'.[14] Archer's attack on the Elizabethan theatre, which he considered primitive and naive, was launched under the influence of naturalism, and it was not successfully refuted until the 1930s. Muriel Bradbrook was foremost among several English critics who insisted that the assessment of Elizabethan drama should not be made to depend on nineteenth century standards of dramaturgy[15], but that the plays should be seen as 'drama sui generis'. This encouraged greater understanding of the soliloquy, and theatricality became a decisive factor in its assessment. Indeed, for the modern playgoer, the question of the psychological probability of a soliloquy seems far less important than whether or not it has the power of conviction and is dramatically effective. Moreover, contemporary drama has once more ceded great significance to the soliloquy – one need only think of monodramas such as Beckett's *Krapp's Last Tape*, where the text consists entirely of the soliloquy of a solitary figure (in itself of course indicative of the isolation of the individual and of his difficulty in communicating with the world around him), or of the lengthy soliloquies in plays by Shaffer, Pinter or Bond. Productions of plays set in a wide variety of styles and eras, such as we are used to seeing on the stage today, help to make us more sympathetic towards the idiosyncrasies of Elizabethan drama than our forefathers were a hundred years ago. What concerns us is not the convention, but the effect which the soliloquy has on us.

Indeed, when the audience or unprejudiced readers encounter one of the great soliloquies, they will sense that here something is finding expression which at this point in time seems so necessary and so convincing that no further justification is needed.

Under such circumstances we do not inquire into the conventions connected with the soliloquy. The soliloquy expresses something which has all the appearance of inevitability and credibility. In many cases we become aware of the fundamental truth that in seeing one character in conversation with another, we only gain a partial and inadequate knowledge of each; we long to know the real person hidden beneath this shell. Or again, we may recognize that something which has been building up over several scenes, without the exact details and intricacies having become quite clear, must be aired and clarified in soliloquy. In the great tragedies it becomes apparent in the soliloquies more than anywhere else that, concurrent to the sequence of outer events, there always runs a sequence of inner events, the one mirroring the other. It is with this in mind that Shakespeare lets his soliloquies confirm what the audience and reader already know, fulfilling at once the expectations of the audience and the demands of dramatic art.

Yet the weight of conviction and the particular impact of a soliloquy can never be explained by a single ingredient, but only by the simultaneous effect of several. The following chapters attempt to show the great variety of devices used by Shakespeare in this respect. A closer investigation of the matter soon reveals that the soliloquy requires a specific approach, and that it is more likely to yield up its secrets to our understanding if we look at it from different angles and in different contexts.

What, then, are the appropriate questions and considerations that will enable us to gain insight into the complexities of the soliloquy and its dramatic effects? The following pages contain some guidelines. It goes without saying that every question is closely linked with a further one – often with several further ones – and that, therefore, for anything to be singled out must inevitably detract from the complex picture of the work of art as a whole. It is also self-evident that some of these questions apply not only to Shakespeare's plays, but to post-Shakespearean drama also. Yet a comparison of similarities and differences will gradually enable us to see what it is that applies quite specifically to Shakespeare's soliloquies. Since the final summary, forming the Conclusion, will take up these questions again, full comments on individual questions can be dispensed with for the time being.

The distinction becomes apparent when different sets of questions are juxtaposed. Thus, while questions about the outer and inner need for a soliloquy, its function or its subject matter, may equally well be applied to plays by other dramatists, much more can be learnt about the distinctive nature of Shakespeare's dramatic art by examining the way in which a soliloquy is woven into the narrower or broader context, its positioning within the scene and in the plot as a whole, how it has been prepared for by means of dramaturgical devices, or by the actual words spoken by the characters.

The examination of the dovetailing of the soliloquy into its context is of particular significance, because Shakespeare – unlike most of his contemporaries – tends most often to introduce his soliloquies in the middle of scenes; soliloquies at the beginning and end of a scene, though they do occur, are less frequent. A comparable distinction becomes apparent when, after investigating the use made of a soliloquy in revealing plans, decisions, conflicts or emotions, we look more closely at the awareness of time, at the soliloquy's commentary on past events and their evaluation. This is particularly relevant for Shakespeare. Does the soliloquy make the audience or the reader see what has just been experienced in a different light, resulting in a different assessment of the situation, or indeed of the character? And do such perspectives, attributable to a considerable degree to the soliloquies, continue to change during the play?

Consideration of Shakespeare's 'mirror-technique'[16] leads on to yet another field of inquiry which is particularly fruitful in connection with Shakespeare's soliloquies: how do the words of the soliloquies conjure up before our eyes the immediate and distant surroundings, the scenery, the atmosphere?

Many dramatists took pains to make the soliloquy dramatic, to free it from the monotony of mere declamation. What means of dramatization, of dialogue within the monologue, did Shakespeare, the instinctive dramatist, discover for himself? Here too there will be many answers, especially concerning the partner in the internal dialogue. This touches the vital nerve of the Shakespearean soliloquy, for there are very few soliloquies in any of his plays where there is no 'partner'.

We also have to consider the link between the dialogue within the monologue and the use of gestures and movements by the actors. An attentive reader will be surprised to see how many hints and directions for the actor are contained in the text of a Shakespeare soliloquy.

All these observations merge ultimately in the preeminent question of the language of the soliloquies. What stylistic devices, what levels of speech, what diction, what kinds of metaphor does Shakespeare use in order to convey all that is required by the content, by the ebb and flow of mind and spirit, by the character of the speaker? The answers to these questions will be far more finely differentiated than they would be if the same questions were applied to the soliloquies of classical German or French drama. The examination of the language will make it particularly clear that we have before us an apparently inexhaustible abundance of creative possibilities.

Moreover, every new soliloquy seems to disclose new features, and to enable us to gain further insights. It may seem to the attentive reader that Shakespeare's soliloquies take on a crystalline quality yielding, more than almost any other element of the plays, a means of access to his dramatic genius.

2

Soliloquies from the history plays

RICHARD III
RICHARD II
KING JOHN
HENRY IV

The first two soliloquies discussed in this chapter are from *Richard III*. In this play Shakespeare discovered new ways of presenting the soliloquy, inspired, no doubt, by the fascinating character of his protagonist and by the need to find appropriate means of expression for Richard's self-dramatization. In order to appreciate the advance made between the soliloquies in the three parts of *Henry VI* and the astonishing monologue in the last Act of *Richard III*, we would have to take a closer look at the trilogy, written only shortly before *Richard III*. For the most part the soliloquies in these history plays still follow established dramatic conventions. They provide the audience with information, epic insets, straightforward declarations of intent, or rhetorical lament, and do not differ fundamentally from the other speeches of the main characters in these plays.[1] There is little inner movement and change. It is only in Richard Gloucester's soliloquy in the third part of *Henry VI* (III.ii.124 ff.) that we find that blend of harsh cynicism and richness of metaphor that is characteristic of the protagonist's speeches in *Richard III*.

In subsequent histories such as *Richard II* and *Henry IV* we can observe each soliloquy growing out of a situation, as well as being interwoven with stage business. Here Shakespeare uses monologue increasingly as a flexible instrument of self-expression. The soliloquies of the Bastard in *King John* have to fulfil a different function, in keeping with his special role as commentator in the play.

As a rule, thinking takes precedence over feeling in the soliloquies in *Richard II* and *Henry IV*. Thought is presented as neatly arranged circumspect argument by a speaker in control of his emotions. It is chiefly in the tragedies that we encounter great eruptions of spontaneous feeling, the fusion of emotion with thought, the excitingly abrupt change from poetic to colloquial language.

Falstaff's ironical and witty monologue on honour, with which this chapter ends, offers the greatest possible contrast to the soliloquies of the king and the prince in *Henry IV*. It belongs to a different category and leads on to the soliloquies of the comedies.

Richard III

ENTER RICHARD, DUKE OF GLOUCESTER, SOLUS
I.i.1–41

Rich. Now is the winter of our discontent
    Made glorious summer by this son of York;
    And all the clouds that lour'd upon our House
    In the deep bosom of the ocean buried.
    Now are our brows bound with victorious wreaths,   5
    Our bruised arms hung up for monuments,
    Our stern alarums chang'd to merry meetings,
    Our dreadful marches to delightful measures.
    Grim-visag'd War hath smooth'd his wrinkled front:
    And now, instead of mounting barbed steeds   10
    To fright the souls of fearful adversaries,
    He capers nimbly in a lady's chamber,
    To the lascivious pleasing of a lute.
    But I, that am not shap'd for sportive tricks,
    Nor made to court an amorous looking-glass;   15
    I, that am rudely stamp'd, and want love's majesty
    To strut before a wanton ambling nymph:
    I, that am curtail'd of this fair proportion,
    Cheated of feature by dissembling Nature,
    Deform'd, unfinish'd, sent before my time   20
    Into this breathing world scarce half made up—
    And that so lamely and unfashionable
    That dogs bark at me, as I halt by them—
    Why, I, in this weak piping time of peace,
    Have no delight to pass away the time,   25
    Unless to spy my shadow in the sun,
    And descant on mine own deformity.
    And therefore, since I cannot prove a lover

To entertain these fair well-spoken days,
I am determined to prove a villain,   30
And hate the idle pleasures of these days.
Plots have I laid, inductions dangerous,
By drunken prophecies, libels, and dreams,
To set my brother Clarence and the King
In deadly hate, the one against the other: 35
And if King Edward be as true and just
As I am subtle, false, and treacherous,
This day should Clarence closely be mew'd up
About a prophecy, which says that 'G'
Of Edward's heirs the murderer shall be—   40
Dive, thoughts, down to my soul: here Clarence comes.

The great opening soliloquy, delivered in prologue-like
fashion by Richard alone on the stage, provides dramatic
exposition and informs the audience about the initial
situation; but at the same time it enables the protagonist to
reveal some of his plans for the future and to give us some
intimation of the role he is going to play. For all of this,
models and established types can be found in pre-
Shakespearean drama, so that in this soliloquy we see
Shakespeare availing himself of several existing traditions.[2]
However, instead of simply making use of one single type at
a time, he combines within a relatively short passage
different functions of the soliloquy, which in earlier plays
were usually kept separate. However, the three basic types
which we recognize here (survey of the situation, self-
introduction, indication of intentions) are not yet inter-
laced with one another; each is contained within its own
separate section. In the soliloquies of the later plays, by
contrast, there is usually a pattern of interconnections
between syntax and content.

In the first thirteen lines the political situation is
presented, as is to be expected in the exposition of an
historical drama. Nevertheless, even in this first general

survey, which employs conventional features of the epic–descriptive style, Richard Gloucester's account is not as objective as would have been expected by pre-Shakespearean standards, but is coloured by subjective sentiment. When Richard speaks of this 'glorious summer', which has been ushered in by 'this son of York', the word *this* (referring to his brother Edward) has a disparaging ring. The proclamation of a coming time of peace in which all strife is going to be buried (1–8) is misleading and grimly ironical. It is also here that we are given a first taste of Richard's spite, when he refers to the lack of manhood in his as yet unnamed brother: 'He capers nimbly in a lady's chamber / To the lascivious pleasing of a lute' (12–13). The stately and ceremonious tone, with its conspicuous use of hyperbole, suggests an undercurrent of irony and malice.

The motives for his villainy which Richard gives at the end of the following section (28–31) follow the pre-Shakespearean tradition of self-description which occurs above all in the monologues of the Vice, one of the stock figures of the morality plays. At the same time the physical deformity which Richard refers to with such self-deprecating wit has been used by many critics and by most actors to provide some 'Freudian' explanation for his twisted personality. However, Richard freely *chooses* to be a villain; the idea that a warped body absolves its owner from the moral responsibility for his evil acts is a modern concept, not an Elizabethan one. It is the circumstance, that he is an outsider from birth, set apart from others by his physical defect, that invests this opening soliloquy with its special credibility.

Richard's self-portrait shows clearly that for him self-observation is a fascinating activity. The sevenfold occurrence of the word 'I' in this section suggests that the speaker can hardly cease looking at himself. His negative comments about himself are hammered into the extended sentence structure with its cumulation of participial constructions. They accelerate the pace of the speech and convey to us his inner impatience, bitterness and sense of outrage. Even within the self-descriptive convention Richard's own true voice is speaking to us in these lines. It is both appropriate and gratifying that the character who is going to manipulate the action in secret should make himself known to us from the start, and should take us into his confidence at least to a certain degree. Of course all this is still done in a straightforward manner typical of Shakespeare's early plays; Richard speaks as if he were observing himself and painting his own portrait. His speech contains a number of indirect stage directions: he displays his deformity to us (14), he looks at his own shadow (26). He will continue to appear as the born play-actor, making the most of a dazzling series of roles: loving brother, jovial uncle, passionate lover, offended friend and – most brilliantly staged of all – the saintly recluse, pretending to refuse the crown offered to him by the Lord Mayor.[3]

With his concluding remarks, in which he announces his stratagem against Clarence, Richard continues a tradition of 'plotting' soliloquies. Yet it is worth noting that on this important occasion of his first appearance Richard does not actually betray his principal aim, although he presents himself to the audience as one who has no place for concealment. There is no mention of his lust for power, which is the hidden motive for his other crimes, so that we are given only a partial insight into his true nature.

The opening scenes of the *Henry VI* trilogy were still encumbered with the exposition of historical, political and genealogical detail. In *Richard III* Shakespeare avoids such ponderous chronicling of facts. Although the soliloquy contains several references to the past and glimpses into the future, the main emphasis is on the figure of the protagonist who emerges as a personality, unmistakably himself. That the Renaissance discovered and portrayed the lone individual aware of his isolation is a well-known fact of cultural history – here is a concrete example. 'I am myself alone' – this sense of otherness, of isolated self-absorption, which Richard Gloucester had tersely formulated towards the end of the earlier trilogy (*3 Henry VI*, V.vi.83), continues to be a keynote of his soliloquies in *Richard III*.

Never again did Shakespeare choose to open a play in so direct a manner – with a soliloquy in which the hero introduces himself and provides the audience with necessary information. In fact there has never been another villain of this sort, licensed from the beginning to dominate the stage and act as puppeteer observing his own feats with such wry amusement. Perhaps Shakespeare recognized the excessive demands that this kind of self-revealing soliloquy makes on the individual actor, who has no previous material to fall back on in developing his role. However, stage history tells us that Richard's first entrance has traditionally been one of the highlights of the play. Before a single word has been spoken, actors like David Garrick, Laurence Olivier, or, more recently, Antony Sher, have been able to establish Richard's personality by means of gesture, movement and facial expression.[4]

RICHARD AWAKES FROM HIS NIGHTMARE – HIS LAST SOLILOQUY
V.iii.178–207

Richard starteth up out of a dream.
K. Rich. Give me another horse! Bind up my wounds!
  Have mercy, Jesu!—Soft, I did but dream.
  O coward conscience, how dost thou afflict me!   180
  The lights burn blue; it is now dead midnight.
  Cold fearful drops stand on my trembling flesh.
  What do I fear? Myself? There's none else by;
  Richard loves Richard, that is, I and I.
  Is there a murderer here? No. Yes, I am!   185
  Then fly. What, from myself? Great reason why,
  Lest I revenge? What, myself upon myself?

Alack, I love myself. Wherefore? For any good
That I myself have done unto myself?
O no, alas, I rather hate myself   190
For hateful deeds committed by myself.
I am a villain—yet I lie, I am not!
Fool, of thyself speak well! Fool, do not flatter.
My conscience hath a thousand several tongues,
And every tongue brings in a several tale,   195
And every tale condemns me for a villain:
Perjury, perjury, in the highest degree;
Murder, stern murder, in the direst degree;
All several sins, all us'd in each degree,
Throng to the bar, crying all, 'Guilty, guilty!'   200
I shall despair. There is no creature loves me,
And if I did, no soul will pity me—
And wherefore should they, since that I myself
Find in myself no pity to myself?
Methought the souls of all that I had murder'd   205
Came to my tent, and every one did threat
Tomorrow's vengeance on the head of Richard.

Richard's last monologue occurs in the fifth Act when he
starts up from the dream in which the ghosts of his victims
have appeared to him.

It is an astonishing piece of self-revelation, second in
importance only to the opening soliloquy from which it
differs in almost every way. Until now Richard has never
examined the workings of his own mind, his sole care has
been the carrying out of his designs, and whatever he has
revealed of his plans and thoughts has been deliberately
controlled. But now, profoundly shaken by the nightmare,
he appears to speak as he is experiencing the shock and to
express thoughts emanating from different levels of consciousness. In a relatively short passage a psychological
drama of great immediacy is enacted.[5]

The soliloquy opens with three short exclamatory

sentences, conveying to us the transition from Richard's experience of the dream to wakefulness. The cry of the first line 'Give me another horse!' prefigures the last words of the king: 'A horse! A horse! my kingdom for a horse!' (V.iv.13). It evokes a premonition of the actual circumstances of his final defeat on the battle-field, as does the demand 'Bind up my wounds!' His anguished entreaty 'Have mercy, Jesu!' is the first sign of deep emotion that he has given, but a moment later, now fully awake, he proceeds to accuse his 'coward conscience', admitting that what he has to contend with is not just an illusion, a dream, but something within himself. In the next two lines his attention is shifting to his surroundings. Perceiving that 'the lights burn blue' (also thought to indicate the presence of ghosts), he realizes that the hour is midnight; he takes note of his abnormal state. In his search for a reason for his feelings he has to admit, reluctantly, that he is afraid of himself. These contradictory impulses are expressed in a sequence of disconnected questions, fragmentary exclamations and demands. Whereas before he had never been in any doubt about his own identity, we now become increasingly aware of a split within his personality, of one part of him turning against another. We see him struggling to achieve a better understanding of himself. With his customary logic he seeks to cross-examine himself, but faced with his own questions and demands he falls into self-contradictions and evasiveness. However, in the end the compulsion to admit the truth to himself breaks through his dialectical defences. His exclamation 'Fool, do not flatter' (193) paves the way for the self-indictment which now follows (194–200).

Conscience, a notion alien to Richard as we have come to know him (though one of the keywords of the play[6]), has turned into a mighty prosecutor with a 'thousand several tongues', condemning him as a villain. The catalogue of his 'sins' (another word which Richard has not previously

used in relation to himself), mounts to a horrifying vision –
all these sins, crying 'Guilty, guilty!' (200), throng to the
bar to accuse him. The three laconic words 'I shall despair'
(201) show that all attempts to justify himself have failed.
His despair is deepened by the admission of his complete
isolation: 'There is no creature loves me' (201). Now, as the
end draws near, his defiant self-reliance has become a
curse. The soliloquy ends with what he has dreamt
merging into plausible reality. The souls of those he has
murdered threaten him with mortal vengeance, foreshadowing his final downfall. Richard's terrifying experience is an anticipation of the apocalyptic vision that
Macbeth is to live through in his first great soliloquy
(*Macbeth* I.vii.16–25), but in the later work Shakespeare
reaches deeper levels of consciousness. For there the images
that arise express the hero's spontaneous feelings.
Richard's method of self-interrogation is still dominated
by his intellect; he presents his thoughts rather than his
feelings or visions, even though we may recognize despair
behind these thoughts. Nevertheless, when the limitations
have been conceded, this soliloquy is a bold anticipation of
possibilities that are to be explored fully in the later plays.
It is effective at this point partly because its style and
language distinguish it from the rest of the play, but also
because of the sudden breakdown of Richard's complacent
role-playing which he has sustained with such skill until
this moment. As the nightmare makes its impact, the
villain's cunning masquerade collapses and he stands
before us, as plaintiff and defendant. The records of stage
history show that this turn of events has provided a
particular challenge for great actors. It inspired, for
instance, William Hogarth's portrait of David Garrick as
Richard 'Starting from his dream' (*c.* 1742) which has
been called 'probably the greatest theatre portrait painted
in England'[7]. Hogarth concentrated on Garrick's realistic
horror as he clutches his sword in one hand – a gesture

which was turned into elaborate stage business by later actors. In recent productions this soliloquy has also been turned to account in indicating a schizophrenic state of mind, or megalomania. Ian Richardson, after playing the part at Stratford, remarked in an interview: 'When it comes to that last soliloquy you realize that he is no longer talking to the audience but to this schizoid person, this alter ego, and you trace back through the script to find where this began to happen and when he started shutting out the audience from his confidence. You find it – and this shows Shakespeare's most remarkable insight – from the moment the crown is on his head.'[8]

Richard II

RICHARD II'S PRISON SOLILOQUY
V.v.1–66

Enter RICHARD *alone.*

Rich. I have been studying how I may compare
　　This prison where I live unto the world;
　　And, for because the world is populous
　　And here is not a creature but myself,
　　I cannot do it. Yet I'll hammer it out.   5
　　My brain I'll prove the female to my soul,
　　My soul the father, and these two beget
　　A generation of still-breeding thoughts,
　　And these same thoughts people this little world,
　　In humours like the people of this world;   10
　　For no thought is contented. The better sort,
　　As thoughts of things divine, are intermix'd
　　With scruples, and do set the word itself
　　Against the word,
　　As thus: "Come, little ones"; and then again,   15
　　"It is as hard to come as for a camel
　　To thread the postern of a small needle's eye".
　　Thoughts tending to ambition, they do plot

Unlikely wonders: how these vain weak nails
May tear a passage thorough the flinty ribs
Of this hard world, my ragged prison walls;
And for they cannot, die in their own pride.
Thoughts tending to content flatter themselves
That they are not the first of fortune's slaves,
Nor shall not be the last—like silly beggars   25
Who, sitting in the stocks, refuge their shame,
That many have and others must sit there;
And in this thought they find a kind of ease,
Bearing their own misfortunes on the back
Of such as have before indur'd the like.   30
Thus play I in one person many people,
And none contented. Sometimes am I king,
Then treasons make me wish myself a beggar,
And so I am. Then crushing penury
Persuades me I was better when a king;   35
Then am I king'd again, and by and by
Think that I am unking'd by Bolingbroke,
And straight am nothing. But whate'er I be,
Nor I, nor any man that but man is,
With nothing shall be pleas'd, till he be eas'd   40
With being nothing.
                                    [*The music plays.*]
              Music do I hear?
Ha, ha! keep time—how sour sweet music is
When time is broke and no proportion kept!
So is it in the music of men's lives.
And here have I the daintiness of ear   45
To check time broke in a disordered string;
But for the concord of my state and time,
Had not an ear to hear my true time broke:
I wasted time, and now doth time waste me;
For now hath time made me his numb'ring clock;   50
My thoughts are minutes, and with sighs they jar
Their watches on unto mine eyes, the outward watch,

Whereto my finger, like a dial's point,
Is pointing still, in cleansing them from tears.
Now sir, the sound that tells what hour it is   55
Are clamorous groans which strike upon my heart,
Which is the bell—so sighs, and tears, and groans,
Show minutes, times, and hours. But my time
Runs posting on in Bolingbroke's proud joy,
While I stand fooling here, his Jack of the clock.   60
This music mads me. Let it sound no more;
For though it have holp mad men to their wits,
In me it seems it will make wise men mad.
Yet blessing on his heart that gives it me,
For 'tis a sign of love; and love to Richard   65
Is a strange brooch in this all-hating world.

A soliloquy can have its effect and fulfil an important
function in the dramatic structure of a play even when the
speaker is not undergoing a profound personal experience;
nor need he be involved in discourse with himself. The long
soliloquy spoken by Richard II in the prison cell shortly
before his death reverts to earlier principles of composition.[9] It is as if the speaker were observing himself
objectively from a distance, as in the opening soliloquy of
Richard III. Yet there are considerable differences. Shortly
before this soliloquy, a dialogue has taken place between
Sir Pierce Exton (the regicide) and a servant, making us
aware of the imminent murder (V.iv). While the king
embarks upon his sweeping and fanciful speculations the
audience expect the murder to take place at any moment.
This disparity between the abstract meditations of the
doomed king and the foreknowledge of the audience
invests the soliloquy with a sombre backdrop and an inner
tension. At the same time, with its mixture of narcissism,
metaphorical embellishment of the situation, brooding
reflection and theatricality, the soliloquy is in keeping with
the character of the king as we have come to know it during

the five Acts of the play. Self-exposition combined with self-interpretation give us a final portrait highlighting his characteristics and his tragic fate.

This last soliloquy is important too for the division of sympathies between Bolingbroke and Richard, for in this play, more than in most others, Shakespeare has caused the sympathies of the audience to fluctuate between the two antagonists. As Richard's authority has declined, the sympathy of the audience has gradually turned towards him, just as, conversely, the rise and ultimate victory of Bolingbroke have been accompanied by withdrawal of the audience's affection for him (although these curves have not, of course, been constant). Now – shortly before Richard II passes out of the play – the audience's feeling for this king, the first passive hero of a Shakespeare play, is once more roused to an intense pitch. Thus the soliloquy has a retrospective and reviewing function, but superimposed is an element of preparation and suspense. The proximity of death and the loneliness of the prison cell accentuate the inner loneliness of failure and defeat. In this particular setting the penetrating irony of the histrionic 'Thus play I in one person many people / And none contented' (31–2) brings home to the audience the tragic fate of the king. The very first lines of the lengthy speech already add a touch of irony to the self-analysis of the king who, throughout the play, exploited almost every situation for its poetic potential, indulging in metaphorical comparisons and fanciful reflections. Now at the end he has set himself a task which seems almost too puzzling even for his speculative mind, so inclined to metaphor:

> I have been studying how I may compare
> This prison where I live unto the world. (1–2)

The grammatical form of the first half-line tells us that he has been occupied with this task for some time, that the soliloquy is continuing a process already begun. He labours to construct a chain of thoughts that will make the difficult process of comparison possible – 'I cannot do it. Yet I'll hammer it out' (5).[10] Thus he hits upon the notion that the thoughts are engendered by his soul and his brain. They people 'this little world' (10), which may refer both to the prison cell and to Richard's body, but they do not live at peace with one another and cannot break through the reality of the stone walls of the prison. The complicated sequence of images is spun out further, yielding various possibilities of interpretation, but ultimately it remains an intellectual game that is played for its own sake, and the futility of it, with death so close at hand, will impress itself upon the audience. It is only by degrees that the king is drawn from these speculations to his own person, which he now confronts with clear awareness, though not without sentimental self-pity. The oscillation between abstract reflection, indulged in for aesthetic pleasure, and histrionic self-centredness has already been apparent in earlier scenes, and it presents the actor with a two-fold task, as John Gielgud has noted: 'that of living in his role and at the same time judging his own effects in relation to his fellow players and the audience'[11]. In this play reflection is combined with lyricism, theatricality with metaphorical exegesis. Even in his ultimate and most profound misery the king, endowed with gifts of rhetoric and fantasy, still feels the need to adorn his hopeless situation with beautiful images, clever comparisons and skilfully correlated patterns of thought.

When during the second half of the soliloquy music sounds (directly after the premonitory words 'till he be eas'd / With being nothing' 40–1), this interruption of his lonely monologue again gives rise to general reflections, which then are brought to focus on himself. The music not keeping time leads Richard to contemplate the time he has heedlessly wasted, for which he was reproached in the garden scene (III.iv) – justly, as he now admits. The rhetorical and metaphorical self-projection of the king culminates finally in the intricate image of the clock. While the image of play-acting in the middle section of the soliloquy draws our attention to the illusionary roles played by this king who now looks back upon his life, the image of the clock makes us see the suffering of the defeated human being. One by one, the parts of the clockwork, the movable hands, and the pendulum's sounds and movements are related to actions and gestures of the king. At the same time the audience has a strong sense of time running out since only a few minutes are to elapse before the murder.

The painstaking way in which the thoughts and comparisons in this soliloquy are elaborated (as, for instance, in the comparison between the dial's point and the finger with which Richard wipes the tears from his eyes), is typical of Shakespeare's early style. The deliberate, distanced manner, too, in which Richard becomes his own observer, interpreter and commentator is in the style of the early and middle plays. None the less, this soliloquy in the prison cell turns out to be a scene of great dramatic importance and intensity, because the setting and the inner situation relate to one another, and the mind and spirit of the king are epitomized in the activity most characteristic of him.

This, the king's only soliloquy, is also one of the longest soliloquies in Shakespeare's plays. It is the final stage in a development which has been discernible in Richard's speeches since the third Act, for he addresses his words less and less to the other characters on stage and becomes increasingly drawn into the ornate representation of his own situation; as a result he often loses sight of other people. At the same time it becomes apparent that this development towards self-orientation is also a process of increasing self-knowledge. In the prison cell Richard shows himself to be a different person from the wayward monarch of the first Acts. The consciousness of his own tragic situation is linked with contemplation of the past and of the future. This adds to the audience's perspectives and influences their assessment of the total situation. When we compare *Richard II* with Marlowe's *Edward II*, it is this soliloquy, in particular, that makes us aware of differences in the characterization of the main figures and in the principles of dramatic composition.[12]

King John

THE BASTARD AS COMMENTATOR

The Bastard in *King John* is another character whose soliloquies strike us as being an inevitable part of his role and of his disposition, for he appears to us from the beginning as an outsider who sees through the other characters and their activities with a keen eye and a mixture of sarcasm and superiority, and who comments on what he sees. His openness and candour, which strike us from the start, make him a particularly credible commentator on the action of the play. His bastardy accounts for his being different and gives him inner independence. In the person of the Bastard, Shakespeare has introduced a spectator into the play, who sees the events differently from those who act them out.[13] Thus the audience may see things twice, first from the viewpoint of the conflicting parties, but then with the critical eye of the Bastard; this leads to an ongoing process of comparison. The Bastard, although he is involved in the action and is sympathetic towards some of the agents, nevertheless is able to comment on it with greater detachment than are those who are directly enmeshed in political intrigue and the struggles for power. The soliloquy is singularly well suited to conveying this sense of aloofness and superiority. The choric function of the soliloquy in pre-Shakespearean drama is evident again here in a refined form appropriate to the keen intelligence of the Bastard, who is able to analyse the driving forces behind the shady actions of those around him.

HIS SPEECH ON COMMODITY

II.i.561–98

[*Exeunt all but the Bastard.*]

Bast.   Mad world! mad kings! mad composition!
   John, to stop Arthur's title in the whole,
   Hath willingly departed with a part:
   And France, whose armour conscience buckled on,
   Whom zeal and charity brought to the field   565
   As God's own soldier, rounded in the ear
   With that same purpose-changer, that sly divel,
   That broker, that still breaks the pate of faith,
   That daily break-vow, he that wins of all,
   Of kings, of beggars, old men, young men, maids,   570
   Who, having no external thing to lose
   But the word "maid", cheats the poor maid of that,
   That smooth-fac'd gentleman, tickling commodity,
   Commodity, the bias of the world,
   The world, who of itself is peised well,   575
   Made to run even upon even ground,
   Till this advantage, this vile drawing bias,
   This sway of motion, this commodity,
   Makes it take head from all indifferency,
   From all direction, purpose, course, intent: 580
   And this same bias, this commodity,
   This bawd, this broker, this all-changing word,
   Clapp'd on the outward eye of fickle France,
   Hath drawn him from his own determin'd aid,
   From a resolv'd and honourable war,   585
   To a most base and vile-concluded peace.
   And why rail I on this commodity?
   But for because he hath not woo'd me yet:
   Not that I have the power to clutch my hand,
   When his fair angels would salute my palm;   590

But for my hand, as unattempted yet,
Like a poor beggar, raileth on the rich.
Well, whiles I am a beggar, I will rail
And say there is no sin but to be rich;
And being rich, my virtue then shall be   595
To say there is no vice but beggary.
Since kings break faith upon commodity,
Gain, be my lord, for I will worship thee!   [*Exit.*]

The soliloquy on commodity is therefore not only an expression of personal opinion, determined by the speaker's disposition and perceptions, but also a commentary applicable to the whole play, outlining its central theme. Yet this does not mean that the Bastard becomes a mere mouthpiece of the author, for his strictures on commodity reveal that he knows that he is immune to its temptations (589 ff.); thus he includes himself in his indictment of human weakness.[14]

The placing of this soliloquy at the end of a long scene – the longest in the play – makes it particularly apt as commentary and résumé, as a mirror in which the preceding events may be shown from a different angle, but at the same time the speech serves as a prelude and pointer for the future, for the observations about commodity seem to expose the principles underlying the course of events to come. In the language of the soliloquy as in its content, we find individuality, together with features typical of detached commentary. The stormy opening 'Mad world! mad kings! mad composition!' (561) is soon succeeded by a long complex sentence in which the juxtaposed epithets for commodity lead to an increasingly graphic description, as if the initially abstract idea were moving more and more towards concrete expression in the imagination of the speaker. The profusion of definitions for commodity, the personification tending now towards abstract notions, now towards concrete visualization, and the minuteness of detail are typical of the style of Shakespeare's middle period, but the soliloquy is given individual colouring by the colloquial expressions (e.g. 569, 572, 582) and by the sarcastically humorous, almost boisterous, way in which the Bastard comes to grips with the notion of commodity. This causes the soliloquy to have a leavening effect, in spite of its objective and synoptic quality. We recognize the validity of the judgement pronounced here, but at the same time our spirits rise to the sparkling wit and animation of the speaker.

Henry IV, Part Two

SLEEPLESSNESS — THE LOT OF KINGSHIP

III.i.1–31

Enter the KING *in his nightgown, with a* PAGE.

King. Go call the Earls of Surrey and of Warwick;
But ere they come, bid them o'er-read these letters
And well consider of them. Make good speed.

Exit [*Page*].

How many thousand of my poorest subjects
Are at this hour asleep! O sleep, O gentle sleep,   5
Nature's soft nurse, how have I frighted thee,
That thou no more wilt weigh my eyelids down,
And steep my senses in forgetfulness?
Why rather, sleep, liest thou in smoky cribs,
Upon uneasy pallets stretching thee,   10
And husht with buzzing night-flies to thy slumber,
Than in the perfum'd chambers of the great,
Under the canopies of costly state,
And lull'd with sound of sweetest melody?
O thou dull god, why li'st thou with the vile   15
In loathsome beds, and leav'st the kingly couch
A watch-case, or a common 'larum-bell?
Wilt thou upon the high and giddy mast
Seal up the ship-boy's eyes, and rock his brains

In cradle of the rude imperious surge,   20
And in the visitation of the winds,
Who take the ruffian billows by the top,
Curling their monstrous heads, and hanging them
With deafing clamour in the slippery clouds,
That with the hurly death itself awakes?   25
Canst thou, O partial sleep, give thy repose
To the wet sea-boy in an hour so rude,
And in the calmest and most stillest night,
With all appliances and means to boot,
Deny it to a King? Then happy low, lie down!   30
Uneasy lies the head that wears a crown.

In the soliloquies presented so far, direct address of an
imagined figure has only occasionally occurred, but in the
following soliloquies of King Henry IV and his son, Prince
Hal, apostrophe becomes a central principle of composition. It is also of significance in some of the soliloquies
to be considered later, so that a comment on Shakespeare's
revitalizing of this convention seems appropriate. Shakespeare was aware that even in solitude man inclines towards
dialogue and needs a partner with whom he can converse
even if that partner is none other than himself. In the
monologues of classical tragedy apostrophe was a common
device, usually involving the invocation of superhuman
beings. In Senecan drama, which exerted a decisive
influence on pre-Shakespearean tragedy, apostrophe had
been used as one of the rhetorical figures of speech to
express lofty sentiments.[15] Shakespeare turned the rigid
pattern into a vehicle capable of expressing intimate
relationships. In dialogue he also made wide and varied
use of apostrophe: in order to address absent persons,
higher powers and personifications, natural objects and
living creatures, so that often an additional partnership
emerged within the dialogue. But in the soliloquy this
special partnership becomes most significant, and the

direct form of address has its greatest impact, frequently involving movement and stage business. The use of apostrophe contributes to the effectiveness with which Shakespeare's soliloquies, particularly those of his middle and late period, draw our attention to the dramatic significance of concrete situations in their setting.

The soliloquy in which the wakeful king addresses sleep is an impressive example of this, for this dialogue with sleep, which avoids the king although it deigns to lie with his humblest subjects, symbolizes the tragedy not just of this particular king but of kingship in general (see for instance *Henry V*, IV.i.236–90). Shakespeare repeatedly places his tragic heroes in situations which are expressive of their inherent nature, their destiny, and which contain *in nuce* the symbolic significance of whole sequences of events.

When we see the king again, in the following Act (IV.v), he will already bear the mark of death. Here he appears alone, overshadowed by sorrow and care, a solitary man, who, in the seclusion of the night, sees to correspondence and arranges discussions, but cannot find sleep. We may recall the first scene of the play, which opened with the king's words 'So shaken as we are, so wan with care'. The idea of the king burdened by sorrow and care, never being able to rejoice in the victory over Richard II, encountering betrayal and mistrust in his own camp, is constantly given new expression in both parts of the play. Here it is embodied compellingly in the image of the sleepless and lonely king. The soliloquy creates the stage picture and fills it with meaning that extends beyond this moment, for, as so often in Shakespeare, individual destiny has general implications. There is an indication of this in the restricted use of the first person singular. The king speaks of himself only in three lines (6–8), while the general contrast between the unrest of sovereignty and the repose granted to the common people is expressed by means of very detailed images. This comparison, in which sleep is repeatedly apostrophized (5, 9, 15, 18, 26), covers more than twenty lines, so that one might think of it as a digression or a piece of philosophizing.

Indeed there is scarcely any link between these lines and the action, and the play could well be understood without them. They have therefore often been included in antho-logies of purple passages from Shakespeare. Here, as on some other occasions, Shakespeare is formulating general reflections which, though fully integrated in the drama, do not seem to need any network of links with the action. Nevertheless, seen within the context of the whole play, the soliloquy appears to be a focal point, and it lingers in our minds, alerting us to the burden of the ruler's responsibilities.

PRINCE HAL ON THE GLORY AND BURDEN OF THE CROWN
IV.v.19–46

Prince. No, I will sit and watch here by the King.
                              [*Exeunt all but the Prince.*]
Why doth the crown lie there upon his pillow,   20
Being so troublesome a bedfellow?
O polish'd perturbation! golden care!
That keep'st the ports of slumber open wide
To many a watchful night! Sleep with it now:
Yet not so sound, and half so deeply sweet,   25
As he whose brow with homely biggen bound
Snores out the watch of night. O majesty!
When thou dost pinch thy bearer, thou dost sit
Like a rich armour worn in heat of day,
That scald'st with safety. By his gates of breath   30
There lies a downy feather which stirs not:
Did he suspire, that light and weightless down
Perforce must move. My gracious lord! My father!
This sleep is sound indeed; this is a sleep
That from this golden rigol hath divorc'd   35
So many English kings. Thy due from me

Is tears and heavy sorrows of the blood,
Which nature, love, and filial tenderness
Shall, O dear father, pay thee plenteously.
My due from thee is this imperial crown,   40
Which, as immediate from thy place and blood,
Derives itself to me. [*Putting it on his head*] Lo where it
     sits,
Which God shall guard; and put the world's whole
     strength
Into one giant arm, it shall not force
This lineal honour from me. This from thee   45
Will I to mine leave, as 'tis left to me.   *Exit.*

The allegorical situation of the preceding soliloquy, centred round the repeated apostrophizing of sleep, invites
comparison with the soliloquy of Prince Hal at his dying
father's bedside not long afterwards, in which apostrophe
is again a dominant structural element. The reflections of
the wakeful king were an isolated unit, tapping the
allegorical and philosophical depths of the situation, while
the action was suspended. Prince Hal's speech, however, is
closely linked with the action and it is addressed not to a
personification but to the visible crown which is lying
beside the sleeping king. The prince seizes the crown,
addresses his father whom he believes to be already dead,
and leaves the room with the crown upon his head. The
king wakes shortly afterwards, to find that he has been
robbed of the emblem of royalty.[16]

The whole scene has an even more powerful symbolic
impact than the soliloquy of the preceding act. Even if it
were only mimed it would have symbolic force. But the
spoken words make us doubly aware of the complex
significance of the scene; they interpret and enhance what
we see, and provide a link with our recollections of what
has happened earlier on. Thus the lines beginning with 'O
polish'd perturbation!' (23–7), recall the related contrast

between the sovereign's sleeplessness and the subjects' untroubled rest. A second, more general apostrophe ('O majesty!' [27]) epitomizes the crown as the weight of responsibility and sovereign dignity bearing down upon the king's head. The boldly figurative comparison with the heavy armour worn in the heat of the day (29) is followed immediately by close attention to present detail: the downy feather is no longer stirred by the king's breath, whereupon Hal concludes that his father is dead. This perception starts off a new chain of thoughts and further resolutions, but these too are made with reference to the visible crown and accompanied by symbolic gestures (42).

The scene is not only a climax in the development of the relationship between father and son, it also affirms in eloquent and emphatic terms the fundamental concern of the whole play.[17] It marks the incipient rise of the prince, who takes upon himself with the crown the great obligations of kingship, thereby completing the process of change which has been subtly initiated in the preceding scenes. A most decisive moment in the tetralogy, bound up with the past and yet decisive for the future, is conveyed in this soliloquy, by means of the momentous words and the symbolism of actions reflecting the resolution of the prince.

The awaking king, however, sees what is happening in quite a different light, and thinks that he has been robbed and deceived when, in fact, the incident represents the fulfilment of his parental wishes. Only after a lengthy confrontation with the prince does he come to see the truth of the matter. This results in one of those ironical Shakespearean situations in which an additional element of tension is derived from the contrast between what the audience already know and what is assumed by those on stage. A recapitulation of what has been said and done becomes necessary, in the course of which the prince repeats his speech to the crown (158–64), though in different words. The commanding position of the soliloquy at the beginning of the scene is thus reinforced by what follows, with the dialogue frequently reflecting the content of the earlier speech. The soliloquy provides the motive force for the ensuing confrontation, and in consequence our recollection of it does not fade, but is consolidated as it recedes further from us.

Henry IV, Part One

FALSTAFF'S REFLECTIONS ON HONOUR
V.i.125–41

Falstaff. I would 'twere bed-time, Hal, and all well.   125
Prince. Why, thou owest God a death.   [*Exit.*]
Falstaff. 'Tis not due yet, I would be loath to pay him
   before his day—what need I be so forward with
   him that calls not on me? Well, 'tis no matter,
   honour pricks me on. Yea, but how if honour prick   130
   me off when I come on, how then? Can honour set
   to a leg? No. Or an arm? No. Or take away the grief
   of a wound? No. Honour hath no skill in surgery
   then? No. What is honour? A word. What is in that
   word honour? What is that honour? Air. A trim   135
   reckoning! Who hath it? He that died a-
   Wednesday. Doth he feel it? No. Doth he hear it?
   No. 'Tis insensible, then? Yea, to the dead. But will
   it not live with the living? No. Why? Detraction
   will not suffer it. Therefore I'll none of it. Honour is   140
   a mere scutcheon—and so ends my catechism.   *Exit.*

Falstaff's soliloquies differ greatly from one another. His complex personality, operating on many different levels, and the inexhaustible richness of his language are reflected in this variety. Each soliloquy has a different style and register. The great soliloquy in Act IV reveals his dubious recruiting practices and presents graphic descriptions of prevailing conditions, as well as realistic portraits of certain types of people and their activities. The vivid picture created is of the wretchedness of a campaign quite without glory and splendour. By contrast, in the soliloquy on honour, he does not refer to any personal experiences, but for the first time analyses an abstract notion. This involves a different style and language: not elaborate figurative descriptions embellished with concrete detail, but concise questions and answers which follow one another in rapid succession, in the manner of a catechism, seemingly irrefutable in their logic. Falstaff himself uses the word 'catechism' to describe his approach; it is the final word in the soliloquy.

It is no accident that this famous soliloquy does not occur until the last Act of the play; we need to know Falstaff in order to appreciate the mood which gives rise to the speech, and to respond accordingly. We need to have experienced this incomparable man during several Acts, to have seen what he does and how he reacts, how he comments on others and is in turn characterized by them. We also learn what powers of observation, mimicry and parody he has, and how with his verbal wit he provides the humorous and yet critical counterbalance to the serious action of the play. It is in this balance that the art and the particular charm of the *Henry IV* plays lie. Only when we have recognized the reality vested in Falstaff as a necessary perspective of the world of the play can we fully understand the speech on honour, which is intended to be simultaneously comic and serious. We must also have learnt something of the dubious world of war, to which this concept of honour belongs, and of the false claims and excesses of the men serving this ideal; otherwise we would not know against whom this exposure of military honour is directed, nor would we recognize that its application is not general, but quite specific.

> By heaven, methinks it were an easy leap,
> To pluck bright honour from the pale-fac'd moon
> (I.iii. 199–200)

It is with these words that Percy Hotspur, in some ways
Falstaff's counterfigure, though in other ways rather
similar to him, gives expression in the first Act to his
military ambitions. 'Thou art the King of honour' is
Douglas's greeting on the eve of the great battle. While
military glory is invoked, not just by Percy Hotspur, but
here and at other points in the scenes preceding Falstaff's
soliloquy, there are also indications enough of the sombre,
inglorious and horrifying aspect of war in this play. As a
civil war it was a reflection of the inner divisions of the
nation, and it was bound to strike the Elizabethan
audience as a warning, as a very real danger that might
threaten the country again. Thus the audience's attitude
to war is already mixed, and Falstaff's soliloquy is aimed
unerringly at this ambivalence. The speech comes at the
end of a scene (in the king's camp near Shrewsbury) which
is already pessimistic in tone. Not for nothing does the king
speak of 'this churlish knot of all-abhorred war' (V.i.16),
and there is an unmistakable undertone of disappointment
and doubt in the negative course of the whole discussion
between the king and Worcester.

During most of this serious conversation, in which
Prince Hal also participates, Falstaff remains silent, but his
presence is a constant reminder that besides the complicated world of warfare there is also that other view of life
which makes it possible to respond to these serious and
tragic events with smiles and irony. He makes only one
sarcastic comment, which immediately provokes the
rebuke of the prince ('Peace, chewet, Peace!' [29]), but
this is enough to provide a flash of awareness of his
presence, before he steps into the foreground at the end of
the scene. The transition from the grave and ominous
discussion of the affairs of state to the light-hearted
conclusion of the scene is accomplished with great skill by
means of a short exchange between Prince Hal and
Falstaff, in prose instead of verse. The unique friendship

between the two is highlighted once more by the ironical references to the imminent battle, but also by Falstaff's upright wish 'I would 'twere bed-time, Hal, and all well' (125). Are those not words spoken from the heart of many at such times, though perhaps unable to express them with such disarming honesty and directness? Falstaff wins our sympathy by finding words for our own suppressed reactions, but he also takes with him into battle his general distaste for the paying of debts. To the prince's parting words 'Why, thou owest God a death' (126) (with the pun on 'debt'), Falstaff, when he is alone, makes the unruffled reply: 'Tis not due yet, I would be loath to pay him before his day' (127–8), and with this cynical witticism he sets the tone for his soliloquy.

What captivates us in this speech, moving us to laughter but also admiration, even to secret approbation, is the apparently irrefutable logic, the practicality with which Falstaff takes the notion of honour down from its pedestal, exposes it and continues to reduce it *ad absurdum* with cogent arguments and answers until really nothing is left of it. He does this with that blend of common sense, vigour and cynicism, lightning reactions and verbal skills which we have come to know in him, and here too – although it is a matter of abstract notion – he demonstrates his ability to transpose everything into concrete ideas, physical terms, into palpable everyday experiences. This is one source of the comic effect, for it is amusing and intriguing to see how he encroaches more and more on the abstraction with his precise questions which allow no escape, until finally it turns out to be all in the imagination, and melts into thin air. The very fact that honour is impalpable proves that it has no substance – except from the viewpoint of the materialist, of course. But this stout, disreputable man, bent on his own advantage, pleasure and safety, also has a clear and penetrating mind. He is educated, by the standards of the time, and belongs only in part to the underworld; part of him is still Sir John, even if he embodies the lamentable decline of aristocratic knighthood.

It is possible to view the critical dismemberment of the notion of honour within its contemporary setting. Parallels in the literature of the time have been pointed out (Cervantes, Molière, Montaigne, amongst others). This may indeed shed light on the background, but, as so often with Shakespeare, there is no absolute necessity for knowledge of contemporary conditions, because the soliloquy treats a theme which is still relevant for us today, and it can have a direct impact on us without such background knowledge.

But how exactly can this impact be described? It is, above all, heartening and liberating. We notice that Falstaff is addressing us directly, and encroaching on us too, with his gestures, his facial expressions and the brilliant question-and-answer game of the catechism. Whether we want to or not, we are compelled to agree with his deductions, or at least to admire the adroitness, cleverness and speed with which he improvises in this game. As with all his soliloquies, the appearance of the portly figure with its cool and leisurely superiority and hedonistic self-assurance is part of the overall effect. Of course, the soliloquy needs to be *acted* before we can really appreciate it. The fat knight is always a histrionic performer of his own part, but he likes to take on other roles as well when he is describing other people or looking at things from a different angle. In his soliloquy he is also pleading for himself and for his way of life. Because of his many faults and weaknesses, and his immorality, we ought really to reject him, but with regard to this figure Sigmund Freud recognized many years ago that 'the demands of morality must rebound from so fat a stomach', and our condemnation of his person 'is disarmed by a whole series of factors'[18]. Nevertheless, we do not cease to pass judgement:

Falstaff's subsequent mutilation of Hotspur's corpse (V.iv.127) is one of the most shocking moments in the play, all the more poignant because he commits this base act in order to gain the rewards of the honour he claims to despise.

Both the involvement of the audience in this soliloquy and Falstaff's alternative view of the heroic events of the war have precedents in the popular theatre.[19] This popular tradition provided Shakespeare with the figure of the Vice, that mischievous and immoral joker who commented on the dramatic action from a critical distance and maintained his links with the audience by addressing them directly. The construction and arrangement of Shakespeare's stage were particularly favourable for this, but with Falstaff, as so often, Shakespeare goes far beyond all possible precedents and traditions. Whether one looks at the traditional Fool, at the Lord of Misrule or at the *miles gloriosus*, it is apparent that Falstaff is a more complex, multi-faceted character, and is above all more human than any of the possible prototypes.

Does Falstaff's witty and yet serious criticism of the heroic ideals of the belligerent lords actually undermine their ethos? This question becomes important when one considers the lasting, as opposed to immediate, effects of the soliloquy on the audience, and there are several possible answers. Clearly the soliloquy raises certain doubts in our minds concerning honour, not only in war, or in a soldier's life, but in life in general. There are traces of this speech later in the play. Honour is returned to at several significant points (V.iii.2; V.iii.33; V.iii.59–60), recalling what we have previously heard in so compact and compelling a form. In this soliloquy we also see the first traces of the disillusionment which is to overshadow the last scenes of the play and is still to be found in the second part of *Henry IV*. Moreover, the soliloquy is directly relevant to the action; Hotspur will obey his idealized notion of honour although this is nonsensical in view of the paucity of his troops; he is felled by the Prince's sword, a victim of his own misguided idea.[20]

Yet we must not forget that whenever we come to one of the serious scenes in the play, concerned with military virtues, the responsibilities of the monarch and other such matters, Shakespeare transposes us straight into this world in such a way that we seem to become entirely involved in it – at least for the duration of such scenes. The two worlds, that of the king and his retinue and that of Falstaff, are not mutually exclusive, but rather they coexist, and are both part of the same great tapestry. Without this soliloquy, without Falstaff and his companions, the play would not only be poorer, it would also be further removed from life and from reality.

3

Soliloquies from the comedies and romances

TWO GENTLEMEN OF VERONA
TWELFTH NIGHT
ALL'S WELL THAT ENDS WELL
MEASURE FOR MEASURE
CYMBELINE
THE TEMPEST

The wide range of mood and atmosphere in Shakespeare's comedies and romances, varying from abandoned merriment, grotesque comedy and delicate irony to the seriousness of self-discovery, is matched by a corresponding diversity in the soliloquies. The passages presented here are a small selection only; they begin with the delightful scene between Launce and his dog in *Two Gentlemen of Verona* and end with Angelo's great soliloquy in *Measure for Measure*, in which he becomes devastatingly aware of his own true nature. Falstaff's speech on honour from *Henry IV* has already been found to have affinities with the typical monologues of the comedies, evoking an amused critical response, and encouraging the audience to laugh but also to think. The romances, Shakespeare's last plays, also contain soliloquies in a variety of styles and structures, yet they do not have the same impact or complexity as the soliloquies of the tragedies which preceded them. For this reason only one speech by Iachimo from *Cymbeline* and one by Prospero from *The Tempest* have been included.

Two Gentlemen of Verona

LAUNCE AND HIS DOG
II.iii. 1–32

   Enter LAUNCE [*with his dog Crab*].

Lau. Nay, 'twill be this hour ere I have done
 weeping. All the kind of the Launces have this very
 fault. I have received my proportion, like the
 prodigious son, and am going with Sir Proteus to
 the Imperial's court. I think Crab my dog be the 5
 sourest-natured dog that lives: my mother weeping; my father wailing; my sister crying; our maid
 howling; our cat wringing her hands, and all our
 house in a great perplexity; yet did not this cruel-
 hearted cur shed one tear. He is a stone, a very 10
 pebble stone, and has no more pity in him than a

dog. A Jew would have wept to have seen our parting. Why, my grandam, having no eyes, look you, wept herself blind at my parting. Nay, I'll show you the manner of it. This shoe is my father. No, this left shoe is my father; no, no, this left shoe is my mother; nay, that cannot be so neither. Yes, it is so, it is so: it hath the worser sole. This shoe with the hole in it is my mother; and this my father. A vengeance on't, there'tis. Now, sir, this staff is my sister; for, look you, she is as white as a lily, and as small as a wand. This hat is Nan our maid. I am the dog. No, the dog is himself, and I am the dog. O, the dog is me, and I am myself. Ay; so, so. Now come I to my father: 'Father, your blessing.' Now should not the shoe speak a word for weeping; now should I kiss my father; well, he weeps on; now come I to my mother. O that she could speak now, like a wood woman! Well, I kiss her. Why, there 'tis: here's my mother's breath up and down. Now come I to my sister: mark the moan she makes. Now the dog all this while sheds not a tear; nor speaks a word; but see how I lay the dust with my tears.

Launce's monologue occurs in one of Shakespeare's first comedies. Unlike classical European drama it conveys neither introspection nor revelation of secrets, neither confession nor isolation. Nor is it necessitated by the plot; it yields no essential new motif in the action. Nevertheless, this is one of the highlights of the play, a culmination of dramatic comedy, as well as an indispensable element of counterpoint in the play's balance. Here Launce, servant and clown, makes his first appearance, introducing himself to the audience. He enters with his dog and stages a heart-rending farewell scene, which at the same time is funny enough to make the audience burst into side-splitting laughter – a scene in which his dog, his shoes and his stick, as well as he himself, play their parts. He not only stages this scene, he also becomes his own observer, co-opting the audience as his confederates in the comedy which he has himself created.[1] During this scene we not only laugh at the figure on the stage, we also laugh with him, while he is deliberately sharing his merriment with us. This is not all, for what Launce is presenting to us in this speech is a corrective, a critically ironical perspective appealing to our sense of reality, in contrast with what has just been occurring among the aristocratic lovers of the main plot. In particular the stylized oaths of love spoken by Proteus will soon prove to be hollow.

Of course there are different levels of possible response and understanding at this point. The naïve spectator with no particular expectations will first of all heave a sigh of relief when the elaborate lovetalk of the preceding scenes is followed by so light an interlude, which cannot fail to amuse even though the relevance of its finer points may not be appreciated. Up to now, although we have been watching a comedy for five whole scenes, the comic element has been provided only by Speed, the other servant-clown in the play. Now at last, with this tardy interlude, there is something to laugh at. Thus the naïve spectators will hardly ask why it is that Launce gives so circumstantial an account of a farewell scene which has just taken place in his family, an event which has little enough to do with the plot of this comedy. They will, however, realize that Launce is a crafty fellow who knows exactly what he is about. The critical observers, on the other hand, will realize that Launce's scene sustains and strengthens the counterbalancing irony and parody of the asides of Valentine's servant Speed in two earlier scenes (I.i; II.i); with even closer attention to detail they will be able to pick up verbal and situational parallels to the main plot. The scene follows immediately on the tearful farewell of the two lovers. Julia, previously so eloquent in the exposition of her love, has found her words choked by tears at the moment of parting. At this point Launce enters – also weeping – and reports the tearful leavetaking in his own family, whereby all the members of the family, including the cat ('our cat wringing her hands' [8]), have played voluble parts in the misery. Only the dog (and Launce will draw attention to him several times) has shown himself to be incapable of tender emotions.

In this first part of the soliloquy the excesses of the parody already give ample scope to the skills of the actor, but then, urged on by the audience's laughter at his account of the farewell, Launce sets about heightening the effect still further by re-creating the scene in the second part of the speech with the help of his props – two shoes, the stick and the dog. He plays his own part but at the same time he is the director, and also provides an illuminating commentary on the scene.

The involvement of the audience is made even more explicit than before by the forms of direct address and exhortation ('I'll show you the manner of it'; 'look you'; 'but see' [15; 21;33]). A further source of comedy, not without psychological significance, is the fact that Launce interrupts and corrects himself several times, confuses his own role and that of the dog, and thus casts doubt on his own identity – a correspondence to the change of personality taking place within Proteus.[2] This comic antici-pation of Proteus' change of identity enables us to see how the soliloquy is integrated within the context of the play. The comic effect is enhanced even further when Launce, whom we have just witnessed as a son kneeling before his father, proceeds to shift into the roles of his mother and his sister as he bids them farewell, imitating the heavy breathing of his mother ('here's my mother's breath' [30]) and the sighing of his sister ('mark the moan she makes' [31]). The flow of gestures and facial expres-sions, combined with the flexibility of language, with constant changes in tempo, adapting to a diversity of registers and roles, offer both a great challenge and opportunity to the actor playing the part of the clown.

The audience will hardly realize to what extent the words and actions on which so much depends in the prose monologue draw on certain rhetorical devices. Shakespeare's masterly handling of rhetorical figures includes the inconspicuous use of them where they would be least expected. Here, for instance, in the first part of the speech, the five consecutive and symmetrically patterned participles help to heighten the comic effect, postponing until the lengthy concluding clause of the long period the introduction of the wholly unconcerned 'cruel-hearted cur' as the main figure in the family drama.[3] We see this very dog 'unmoved' before us on the stage.

By the time we have witnessed the soliloquies of Launce which follow in the third and fourth Acts (III.i; IV.iv), having previously listened to the conversation of the two servant–clowns in front of the ale-house in Milan (II.v), it will have become apparent that both of these figures, but particularly Launce, contribute something to the play which goes beyond a mere comic interlude. They offer an alternative perspective on what is being enacted on the higher level of the plot. Thus, this early and imperfect comedy already tends towards the multiplicity of view-points distinctive of Shakespeare's middle plays. With the figure of Launce and the powerful involvement of the audience in his monologue Shakespeare is picking up a tradition of popular drama, in particular of the Italian *commedia dell'arte*, in which the sly servant-figures quite frequently appeared on stage accompanied by animals; but whereas those animals served no further purpose than to divert the audience, what is new in Shakespeare is the presentation of the dog Crab as an ironic parallel to the human beings in the play, parodying their behaviour and their speechlessness, but also their ingratitude and lack of feeling. As Alexander Leggatt has pointed out, 'to watch similar events causing emotional crisis in one case, and casual laughter in the other, trivializes the events by removing their uniqueness'.[4] The comic and sarcastic commentaries of the two servant–clowns enable us to observe and laugh at the conventionality and limited vision of the courtly wooing from a viewpoint which we can accept as our own. Thus the monologue is a milestone in the development of Shakespeare's dramatic art, and this bipolar principle of structure has rightly been acclaimed as the point of departure for the unprecedented wealth of contrasts and interconnections in his plays.

This is not the only anticipation of the distinctive characteristics of Shakespeare's later soliloquies. There is also the art of drama employed in the visual re-enactment of the narrative. Shakespeare's soliloquies demand the full range of the actor's skills, implying gestures, properties and tacit partners, changes in tempo, and perhaps in style and register. Another point that distinguishes this type of soliloquy from the soliloquies of pre-Shakespearean drama is their degree of concrete reality and physical immediacy. Some things are presented to us in concrete form (not only the dog, but the shoes, the stick and so on); other non-tangible circumstances of the leave-taking in the house of Launce's parents, for instance, are given a kind of physical reality by the descriptive report and by the re-enactment of the scene. If we were to indicate what is most promising in this play, and where we are struck by the particular quality of Shakespeare's creative genius, we would think, above all, of Launce's soliloquies.

Twelfth Night

MALVOLIO'S APPEARANCE IN THE GARDEN SCENE, WITH EAVESDROPPERS
II.v.143–79

Malvolio. [*Reads*] *If this fall into thy hand, revolve. In my stars I am above thee, but be not afraid of greatness. Some*

are born great, some achieve greatness, and some have 145
greatness thrust upon 'em. Thy fates open their hands, let
thy blood and spirit embrace them, and to inure thyself to
what thou art like to be, cast thy humble slough, and appear
fresh. Be opposite with a kinsman, surly with servants. Let
thy tongue tang arguments of state; put thyself into the trick 150
of singularity. She thus advises thee, that sighs for thee.
Remember who commended thy yellow stockings, and
wished to see thee ever cross-gartered: I say, remember. Go
to, thou art made, if thou desir'st to be so. If not, let me see
thee a steward still, the fellow of servants, and not worthy to 155
touch Fortune's fingers. Farewell. She that would alter
services with thee,
                    The Fortunate Unhappy.
Daylight and champaign discovers not more! This
is open. I will be proud, I will read politic authors, 160
I will baffle Sir Toby, I will wash off gross
acquaintance, I will be point-device the very man.
I do not now fool myself, to let imagination jade
me; for every reason excites to this, that my lady
loves me. She did commend my yellow stockings of 165
late, she did praise my leg being cross-gartered,
and in this she manifests herself to my love, and
with a kind of injunction drives me to these habits
of her liking. I thank my stars, I am happy. I will be
strange, stout, in yellow stockings, and cross- 170
gartered, even with the swiftness of putting on.
Jove and my stars be praised!—Here is yet a
postscript. [*Reads*] *Thou canst not choose but know who
I am. If thou entertain'st my love, let it appear in thy
smiling, thy smiles become thee well. Therefore in my* 175
presence still smile, dear my sweet, I prithee. Jove, I
thank thee, I will smile, I will do every thing that
thou wilt have me.   *Exit.*

The passage presented here as Malvolio's monologue is
actually only the conclusion of his soliloquizing, which

constitutes most of the scene. Whereas up to now his utterances have constantly been interrupted by the comments of the eavesdroppers, at this point Malvolio speaks a lengthy passage without interjections from the hidden observers.

The unfailing comedy of this scene was already noted in Shakespeare's own time, and its popularity is attested by the fact that in the year 1623 a performance of the play at the court of King James I was entered in the Revels Accounts under the title of 'Malvolio'. The effect is based on careful preparation and on the synchronization of various devices of staging and language, amounting to one of the most complicated situations in any Shakespearean soliloquy, made possible by the design of the Elizabethan stage where one actor could be speaking a monologue on the projecting platform, while a dialogue was taking place further back on the stage at the same time, the audience experiencing the interplay of both. That this interplay is – at least by one party – not intended and not observed heightens the comedy. That the situation is moreover improbable and indeed absurd is in line with a well-tried dramatic convention, namely the overhearing of a soliloquy, which Shakespeare here pushes to its uttermost limits.

Shakespeare has not only created a situation in which there are two sets of observers and listeners, ourselves in the auditorium and the actors on the stage; he has also established correspondences and contrasts between both areas of spectators. With their observations the eavesdroppers help us, the audience, to gain a sharper awareness of the role into which Malvolio is launching himself; but although we laugh with them, we remain at a good-humoured distance from them. This applies in particular to Sir Andrew, whose retarded mental metabolism prevents him from participating fully in the gulling; he too is laughed at, and his reaction to Malvolio's dreams of future greatness contributes to the growing suspense, as well as to

our enjoyment of the scene. Sir Toby's outbursts of anger –
he would like best to resort to blows – have to be attenuated
time and again by Fabian, so that the hoax which has been
so carefully prepared shall not be prematurely discovered.
Malvolio notices nothing of Sir Toby's outraged and
increasingly vociferous interjections, but continues un-
abashed and blind in his delusions, and the very improb-
ability of this serves to emphasize the extent of his
absorption and isolation. Thus, in psychological terms,
Shakespeare has turned the unrealistic stage convention to
good account.

Yet our attention is concentrated most of all on the
gulling of Malvolio: will he fall into the trap which Maria
has so cunningly laid for him? Will he readily take the bait?
Will the intrigue be successful in every way? Or will the
victim eventually see through it? As we can see from
Malvolio's soliloquy, everything is to turn out exactly as
planned. Not only does he accept the forged letter as his
mistress's authentic declaration of love, without entertaining the slightest doubt, he also sees in it the fulfilment of his
various fantasies and delusions. His vast self-deception and
presumption help to complete the process set in motion at
the beginning of the scene. We have been prepared step by
step for the expectations with which Malvolio opens the
letter, and then proceeds to read it aloud. The eavesdroppers are ignorant, as we are, of the exact contents of the
letter that Maria has formulated and they listen to the
reading of it as eagerly as we do. Shakespeare, with an eye
to all these details, has arranged for Maria to leave the
stage shortly before.

It is necessary to turn back a few pages in order to
register the full extent of the skilful preparation for the
climax of this soliloquy. Even before Malvolio enters, the
incomparable Maria has been reporting the manner in
which he is projecting himself into his fantasy role, and she
has foretold the effect which the letter will have on him:

he has been yonder i' the sun practising
behaviour to his own shadow this half hour:
observe him, for the love of mockery; for I
know this letter will make a contemplative
idiot of him.

(16–20)

When Malvolio then enters, both his outer appearance
and his state of mind are conveyed in Fabian's words:
'Contemplation makes a rare turkey-cock of him: how he
jets under his advanced plumes!' (27). But then Malvolio
himself takes over the direction of the scene,[5] in bold
anticipation of the projected future in which he imagines
himself already married to Olivia. His wishful thinking
expresses itself not merely in general terms: he stages a kind
of private performance of a scene in the house of his
betrothed, in which even minor details are elaborated,
relishing it with a high sense of his own importance. As the
severe and dignified master of the house, surrounded by
numerous members of the household, he is now in a
position to exert disdainful authority over the undiscip-
lined Sir Toby. What Fabian has just said, 'Look how
imagination blows him' (42–3), Malvolio now demonstrates himself. Even before he finds the love-letter that
has been strategically placed for him, it is already apparent
that for Malvolio it is not a matter of love for Olivia but of
the raising of his social status and the consequent increase
in his power and authority.[6] To become 'Count Malvolio'
is what he really wants (35). When the reading of the letter
actually begins, after the comic deciphering of the salu-
tations and the accompanying notes, made more comic by
the long-winded pedantry of the procedure, we already
know enough about Malvolio's state of mind to appreciate
how close the letter comes not only to his wishes and
designs but also to his style, with its cumbersome latinisms.
In company Malvolio's language is pedantic and lacking
in spontaneity; when he is alone he speaks almost entirely

in inflated, pompous phrases, as if he wanted to give additional emphasis to his newly acquired dignity and unapproachability.

It is in the paradoxical nature of this soliloquy to reveal not what Malvolio is, but what he would like, and is unable, to be. Self-deception and misjudgement of their own potential is a weakness to which almost all the characters in this play succumb, but Malvolio exemplifies it in its most extreme form.

Even without the dramatic situation into which it is fitted this letter would be a very comic document. Solemn exhortation and prophecy are mixed with stilted pomposity and artificiality. It reads not like a declaration of woman's love but like a stiff, somewhat unfriendly and moreover authoritarian epistle, conveying to the reader in admonitory form not only a message of promise and 'advices',[7] but also strict instructions (with unmistakable threats in the event of non-observance) which may be interpreted as a parody on the literalism of the puritans of the day. The transition from the elevated style of the mysterious prophecy 'Some are born great . . .' (in which the rhetorical device of repetition helps the audience to mark the maxims which will be referred to again several times), to the colloquial 'Go to' seems to suggest a certain degree of familiarity, but this will soon turn out to be a feigned familiarity only.

As a love-letter the whole text, which never actually mentions love, is so absurd that the inflated self-estimation of a Malvolio is indeed necessary for it to be read without suspicion and laughter, and for such grave conclusions to be drawn from it.

The letter appeals to the fantasy which Malvolio has already cherished for a long time – the ascent to a lofty position in society from which he will be able to look down with condescension even upon a 'kinsman'. The kinsman is, of course, Sir Toby, who, in his hiding-place, will react to this impudence with a mixture of amusement and rage. Similarly the exhortation 'Let thy tongue tang arguments of state; put thyself into the trick of singularity' (150–1), which encourages Malvolio to abandon himself to his inclinations, will lay him open to further mockery. The instructions for his attire go one step further again, for yellow stockings cross-gartered (a form of dandified finery already out of fashion even with the young at that time) are simply not in keeping with the person of the steward, who has appeared up to now in dignified black garb. This applies even more to the postscript instruction that he should smile, with the malicious supplement 'thy smiles become thee well' (175), for to smile is not in the nature of this humourless man, however much those around him may yield to merriment. Therefore the forced smile which Malvolio attempts at his next appearance not only adds to the comic effect, but also provides a grotesque and thought-provoking contrast within the context of the play as a whole.[8]

Malvolio's soliloquy follows directly on the reading of the letter. Promptly he resolves to implement his mistress's demands, even exceeding what the letter has suggested. There follow five short sentences, each beginning with 'I will', sounding almost like a statement of policy, declaimed in high tones with maximum assurance. Here, too, the prose style which Malvolio adopts is stilted and ponderous, formalistic and pedantically unnatural. Even at the height of good fortune Malvolio talks like a hidebound official, still within the confines of his self. Twelve times the pronoun 'I' is repeated; we become aware that he really is concerned only with himself, and that this self-centredness is the prerequisite for the blindness and wrong-headedness with which he has precipitated himself into the snare prepared for him. He will now continue to act just as Maria has foreseen. Thus in the overall dramatic structure of the play this soliloquy is significant both as fulfilment and confirmation of what has gone before, and as subtle preparation for what is to come: we are seeing a kind of rehearsal for the scenes which are to follow.

Although this is one of Shakespeare's most entertaining scenes, beneath the amusing surface there are basic human issues at stake which prompt us to reflect and to pose questions; it is this questioning which distinguishes Shakespeare's comedies so markedly from those of his contemporaries, with the exception of Ben Jonson. If we are to appreciate fully the dual effect of this soliloquy, we must bear in mind the part that Malvolio plays in the drama as a whole. Although he does not figure in the main plot, he represents from the beginning the sombre and humourless contrast to the joyful world full of music and merriment, in which high spirits were licensed to break through the established order.

In responding to the gulling of Malvolio, the Elizabethan audience may well have seen a connection with the implications of the title, *Twelfth Night*. This will have called to mind the saturnalian celebrations which took place every year between Christmas and the Feast of the Epiphany,[9] when the carnival spirit prevailed, combining practical jokes with the mockery of those in authority, and establishing the supremacy of the Lord of Misrule. The mocking and ridiculing of Malvolio, as steward a person of authority, by the rollicking members of the household could seem to Shakespeare's audience to be in keeping with the spirit of Twelfth Night, and they may well have seen in him a caricature of the contemporary puritan, who was fundamentally opposed to all such drunken exuberance.[10] However, the human issues with which Shakespeare is concerned usually transcend such contemporary frames of reference and can therefore be apprehended by an audience with no such background knowledge.

Even before this scene Malvolio (the 'evil-wisher') exerts his authority as steward with severity, intolerance and humourlessness. Shortly before this scene he had been disturbed by the noise of the jolly bout of drinking that is taking place late at night in his lady's house, and he has come as an extremely unwelcome killjoy to enforce order (II.iii), exercising an authority uncalled for in this situation. Although he is carrying out his duty and protecting the interests of his lady, his self-love, vanity and morose lack of humour, as displayed here, arouse antipathy, and not for the first time; his jarring behaviour and attitudes provoke the plot which is hatched against him. So in this soliloquy the solemn and dignified man becomes an unwitting laughing-stock. We laugh at him whole-heartedly, and we concede that he has deserved this humiliation, even if our pleasure at his discomfiture is not quite so great as that of the eavesdroppers.

Yet this feeling of satisfaction is countered by other reactions. If someone falls unawares into a trap and is mocked by all, we tend to enjoy the comedy but we also feel a certain sympathy for the victim. We don't need to go as far as Charles Lamb 160 years ago when he declared that, particularly with regard to the last Acts, Malvolio must be seen as a tragic figure,[11] and yet we follow his misguided course with mixed feelings. In this soliloquy we are especially aware that behind the comic deciphering of the letter and the no less comic resolve to adopt the new role, there is another dimension: the loneliness and isolation of the egoist enmeshed in self-deception, who has lost touch with the world around him and lost also the capacity for love. His subsequent fate – being imprisoned in a dark cell – makes his isolation increasingly clear. His mounting euphoria, culminating in this soliloquy, strikes us as being very funny, but it also brings home to us the terrible possibilities of human self-delusion. When all is said and done the self-congratulatory man before us is pitiable. That much is clear even before we reach the final Acts.

All's Well That Ends Well

HELENA REVEALS HER HIDDEN LOVE

I.i.75–96, 212–25

Lafew. Farewell, pretty lady; you must hold the credit   75
   of your father.   [*Exeunt Bertram and Lafew.*]
Helena. O, were that all! I think not on my father,
   And these great tears grace his remembrance more
   Than those I shed for him. What was he like?   80
   I have forgot him; my imagination
   Carries no favour in't but Bertram's.
   I am undone; there is no living, none,
   If Bertram be away; 'twere all one
   That I should love a bright particular star   85
   And think to wed it, he is so above me.
   In his bright radiance and collateral light
   Must I be comforted, not in his sphere.
   Th' ambition in my love thus plagues itself:
   The hind that would be mated by the lion
   Must die for love. 'Twas pretty, though a plague,   90
   To see him every hour; to sit and draw
   His arched brows, his hawking eye, his curls,
   In our heart's table—heart too capable
   Of every line and trick of his sweet favour.
   But now he's gone, and my idolatrous fancy   95
   Must sanctify his relics. Who comes here?

✱

Helena. Our remedies oft in ourselves do lie,
   Which we ascribe to heaven; the fated sky
   Gives us free scope; only doth backward pull
   Our slow designs when we ourselves are dull.   215
   What powers is it which mounts my love so high,
   That makes me see, and cannot feed mine eye?
   The mightiest space in fortune nature brings
   To join like likes, and kiss like native things.

Impossible be strange attempts to those   220
That weigh their pains in sense, and do suppose
What hath been cannot be. Who ever strove
To show her merit that did miss her love?
The king's disease—my project may deceive me,   224
But my intents are fix'd, and will not leave me.   *Exit.*

The two soliloquies spoken by Helena in the first scene illustrate the way in which Shakespeare uses the soliloquy in his 'problem comedies' to throw light on the enigmatic personality of the main character, with its complications and conflicts. In this somewhat discordant comedy which is rarely performed and is, in some ways, difficult for a modern audience to understand, it is Helena who is the motive force of both the outer and the inner action. She is a character of some complexity, combining features which are usually seen as opposites; she displays boldness and a high degree of intelligence and will-power, but also modesty, humility, tenderness and charm. She has to accomplish exceptional and difficult tasks; yet her un-wavering love gives her strength to strive towards her apparently unattainable goal with wit and determination.

The motifs of fable and romance derived from the source (such as the miraculous healing of the king, and the union with Bertram made possible by means of disguise and subterfuge) seem incongruous with the psychological realism of Helena's complex personality as displayed in some scenes. This has led to contrasting interpretations of her character.[12] Yet this very blend of divergent and, at times, almost incomprehensible features contributes to the inner tension which is sustained throughout the play, and which provokes certain questions which remain unan-swered – for us more than for an Elizabethan audience that was, on the whole, prepared to accept such romance motifs.

With regard to the second part of the play, which is determined by Helena's unusual and surprising, even disturbing course of action, it was necessary for Shakespeare to find means early on in the play of impressing upon us a vivid image of her character, arousing our interest and our sympathy at the same time. This had to be done with discretion, because at the beginning of the play Helena is still in the background; the action moves forward at first without her help. How does Shakespeare succeed in conveying the impression that the two moments of intimate self-revelation, in which we learn such vital information about Helena, are not isolated instances of self-explanation but integral parts of the action? While, at the beginning of the scene, the Countess, Bertram and Lafew are conversing about the death of the Count and the more recent death of the physician Gerhard of Narbonne, Helena, his daughter, stands in silence. However, the warm-hearted and loving words spoken by the Countess in praise of her, direct our attention towards her and bring tears to her eyes, so that we look at her with interest when, in the course of the conversation, she makes two short remarks which cause us to reflect. What is it that she wants to convey? Her role as a timid bystander, her looks and gestures as Bertram takes his leave of those present, prepare us for the moment when she is alone and can express her feelings.

Her soliloquy is born out of the situation and this makes us quite forget that it is, in fact, the self-presentation and revelation of a new character. With the cry 'O, were that all!' she is still responding to Lafew's parting words 'You must hold the credit of your father' (75–6). It is something different, namely the departure of Bertram, which is actually moving her. At this moment she perceives clearly what the separation from Bertram, who knows nothing of her love, means to her. 'I am undone' (82) she exclaims. Her secret love was fed by the presence of her beloved, by the sight of him. In the bitter-sweet recollection ('Twas pretty, though a plague, / To see him every hour' [90–1]) she memorizes his features and the expression of his face. For a moment we, too, see Bertram, of whom we have so far received only a superficial impression, through Helena's eyes.

The soliloquy, which is so closely linked with the scene that we have just witnessed, emphasizes in clear terms the harsh law according to which the beloved cannot be attained. Helena cannot hope ever to overcome the disparity in social standing which separates her from the Count. Whereas the language of the first part of the soliloquy is marked by brief, even colloquial phrases, by words which she almost seems to be speaking to herself, superimposing natural speech rhythms on the underlying metrical pattern, now the diction is intensified. It leads towards the poetic image which describes the allotted fate in which her love for Bertram has placed her in terms of astronomical constellation. Helena receives the bright radiance of the star circling high above her, takes comfort from it, but cannot move in the same sphere. This image strikes us all the more because of its stylistic context;[13] it is an early indication of the adamantine social barriers existing between Helena and Bertram, barriers which are an essential element in the development of the plot, and which constitute one of the basic themes of the play. In these and the following lines we also observe Helena's intelligence and insight, coupled with her passionate love; above all we see these qualities in the antithesis of the last sentence, with the paradoxical 'idolatrous' (95) and 'sanctify' (96). Helena knows that her love is unending, absolute and unalterable, but she is also able to step back and look at herself from a critical distance, and call her love 'idolatrous'.

The last seven lines of the soliloquy form a transition to the ensuing dialogue. Parolles has entered and Helena prepares us for his part in the scene, indicating the extent to which she sees through his boasting and folly although, with her generous nature, she is prepared to tolerate him. The lines lead up to the dialogue, on which we need to dwell briefly; it prepares us, indirectly, for the very different final soliloquy. In the sarcastic and witty exchange on the value of virginity we see an entirely different side of Helena. With unembarrassed ease she replies to Parolles' questions, some of them ambivalent, without giving anything away and without letting herself be provoked. She shows her quick-wittedness and intellectual calibre in this skirmish with words. At some points we may note, as Parolles is not able to, how much of herself and of her secret love for Bertram she is incorporating into what she says about him and about his future role at court. Her love does not prevent her from seeing Bertram's weaknesses. Beneath the surface of this entertaining conversation something else is going on. We are reminded of what we have just heard in the soliloquy about her hopeless love, but at the same time we notice how her mood has changed while she has been conversing so merrily and wittily. What does this mean? Is she intent on concealing her suffering, or is something new taking shape in her mind and her emotions?

Her final soliloquy (212–25) provides an answer. Helena has taken a decisive step forward: her despair has been replaced by a new-found trust in her capacity to determine her own fate and to make rightful use of the freedom granted her by heaven. Her own feeling reminds her that such boundless love has often achieved the impossible, overcoming great distances and disparities. Almost every sentence spoken in the first soliloquy has a positive counterpart in this second one. Her new vision of the world gives rise to a new plan of action, disclosed to us in the closing lines: to cure the king's disease, and thereby – perhaps – to find a way of winning Bertram after all. She resolves to tread in her father's footsteps, and we recall the parting words of Lafeu preceding her first soliloquy: 'You must hold the credit of your father.' The structure of this final soliloquy is again significant. Instead of the brief restless sentences of the first soliloquy we now hear rhyming couplets. The newly gained insight is moulded into the form of maxims. Metre and language give emphasis and add weight to Helena's firm determination and inner confidence.

If we were to read this final soliloquy out of context, without taking note of the inner development which has preceded it, we might easily understand these apparently dogmatic maxims and aphorisms about life as a statement of the principles underlying the main themes of the play, for which Helena is simply the mouthpiece. Indeed in pre-Shakespearean tragedy the soliloquy was often used for such general purposes. But if, as we have tried to do, we look at the soliloquy in relation to the first scene and with regard to Helena's inner being, we recognize that it represents a highly individual statement on her part, and a new stage of her development.

Measure for Measure

ANGELO DISCOVERS HIS HUMAN NATURE
II.ii.162–87

Isabella. Save your honour.   [*Exeunt all but Angelo.*]
Angelo.   From thee: even from thy virtue!
  What's this? What's this? Is this her fault, or mine?
  The tempter, or the tempted, who sins most, ha?
  Not she; nor doth she tempt; but it is I   165
  That, lying by the violet in the sun,
  Do as the carrion does, not as the flower,
  Corrupt with virtuous season. Can it be
  That modesty may more betray our sense
  Than woman's lightness? Having waste ground enough,
  Shall we desire to raze the sanctuary   171

And pitch our evils there? O fie, fie, fie!
What dost thou, or what art thou, Angelo?
Dost thou desire her foully for those things
That make her good? O, let her brother live!   175
Thieves for their robbery have authority,
When judges steal themselves. What, do I love her,
That I desire to hear her speak again?
And feast upon her eyes? What is't I dream on?
O cunning enemy, that, to catch a saint,   180
With saints dost bait thy hook! Most dangerous
Is that temptation that doth goad us on
To sin in loving virtue. Never could the strumpet
With all her double vigour, art and nature,
Once stir my temper: but this virtuous maid   185
Subdues me quite. Even till now
When men were fond, I smil'd, and wonder'd how.

Exit.

Angelo's soliloquy occurs at the end of the dramatic scene
in which he and Isabella first talk to one another. It is his
first soliloquy, and his longest and most eloquent confession, a turning-point in his inner development and also in
the plot as a whole.[14] During this scene of temptation and
persuasion Isabella repeatedly tries in vain to touch some
chord of human sympathy and understanding in Angelo.
As representative of the absent duke Angelo has re-
introduced a law not enforced for nineteen years. Isabella
begs for clemency for her brother, who has been sentenced
to death according to this law because Julia, to whom he is
as yet not lawfully wed, is expecting his child. Only
towards the end of the scene does Isabella succeed in
piercing Angelo's armour of icy rejection, by challenging
him to knock at his own door and to enquire of his heart

what it does know
That's like my brother's fault

(II.ii.138–9)

A meaningful aside of Angelo's reveals to us that with this she has hit the mark, but at the same time we note that it is not simply the compelling nature of her arguments that has moved Angelo so deeply; rather it is the effect of Isabella herself, her womanly radiance, her purity and beauty. In a second aside Angelo speaks the word that will be the keyword of all that follows: temptation. For a moment we have a sense of what is going on inside him, beneath the surface of the brief answers to Isabella. They indicate his inner dilemma, but we are prepared for the soliloquy not only by this but also by Isabella's general indictment of 'man, proud man' (118), who has lost all awareness of his own frailty. What she intends as an appeal to the Christian virtues of mercy, forgiveness and charity provides an apt supplement to our impression of Angelo, namely that of a man corruptible through his powerful position (111–24).

In order to absorb the full effect of the soliloquy we shall have to recall earlier commentaries on Angelo. He has been spoken of by the duke in laudatory terms: his integrity, his severity towards himself, his exactness in the fulfilment of the law, have been commended. There has already been evidence, without any details being given, of his unrelenting attitude towards all who transgress the law. He has dismissed all possibility of ever yielding to temptation himself (II.i.17–18). To all observers he seems to be impervious to the stirrings of the blood. The duke said of him:

> Lord Angelo is precise;
> Stands at a guard with Envy; scarce confesses
> That his blood flows; or that his appetite
> Is more to bread than stone. Hence shall we see
> If power change purpose, what our seemers be.
>
> (I.iii.50–5)

The adjective 'precise' alludes to the Puritans, who were also named 'precisians' because of their scrupulous adherence to religious prescriptions.[15] The duke's words seem to suggest a danger lying hidden beneath Angelo's puritanical self-righteousness. The note of warning in the last two lines – and there are more such lines – may be rephrased as the question: has Angelo not denied his own self? Will not the moment come for him as for others when this artificial edifice will collapse? And we ask further: what constellation would be necessary in order for this collapse to take place in someone who is apparently more unyielding than all others to human inclinations? During the encounter between Isabella and Angelo we realize that the seemingly impossible can indeed only be achieved in this unique situation, in which Angelo, the all-powerful, is approached by the desperate woman coming to implore his help. Purity and virtue, the very qualities championed by Angelo (whose name is no accident[16]), are combined in Isabella with beauty, intelligence and an aura of mystery. The uniqueness of this encounter between two people who are at once so alike and yet so unalike prepares us for the uniqueness of the soliloquy. We wonder what changes are wrought in Angelo.

We note revealing differences even in the details of the language which he now uses; his agitation is reflected in the syntax and also, unmistakably, in the melody of the speech. For the first time we hear from Angelo not only well-constructed sentences but also repeated exclamations and questions, as well as noticeable pauses between the separate utterances. Angelo's agitation has disrupted the sentence structure, and the precise and controlled diction which has been at his disposal hitherto. With the first complete line of the soliloquy, consisting in itself of two incomplete clauses, Angelo continues to converse with the departed Isabella, ironically extending her parting salutation 'Save your honour' (161), and recalling her earlier 'Heaven keep your honour safe!' (157): so precisely has he taken note of Isabella's words and applied them now to himself, in a sense of which she herself could, of course, have no idea. Then his feelings erupt; the reiterated 'What's this?' gives vent to his horror at himself. He has discovered something in himself which was previously unknown to him, or which he was unwilling to know. Nine times more Angelo's utterances end with question marks, nine times he interrogates himself, enquiring into everything which at first he cannot grasp, and into whatever seems to him nonsensical and paradoxical. Initially he appears to waver as to who is actually to blame for this temptation which has overwhelmed him: he or Isabella? But his intellect and honesty, still remarkable, even later on, force him to abandon the search for ways of escape, and to acknowledge himself to be the sole transgressor.

In a highly suggestive image he compares himself to the carrion lying beside the violet in the sun; he, unlike the violet, is caused to rot by the sun's rays.[17] Does he mean to say that the light radiating from the sun (that is to say, the virtue and purity radiating from Isabella) would by contrast have called forth virtue from another man, who was not, as he was, susceptible to corruption? Since his puritanical attitude makes all sensuousness seem foul desire, his feelings for Isabella are immediately correlated in his mind with sin and vice. The paradoxical realization that, whereas the customary sexual allurements, the seductions of the brothel, exert no power over him (183), the chastity of the pure maid has bewitched him, threads its way through the whole soliloquy. In the second question 'Having waste ground enough . . .' (170) the contrast between Isabella's purity and his corrupt desires are formulated with even stronger self-reproach. Isabella seems to him a sanctuary that he would desecrate. Yet at this point he still recoils before this desecration, as his horrified 'O fie, fie, fie!' (172) makes plain.

In the terse self-interrogation in the middle of the soliloquy, Angelo confronts himself, subjects himself to self-scrutiny and shudders at what he sees. Here the self-address that in earlier monologues tended to be a mere rhetorical formula, has become an inevitable necessity. It is the first time that the question 'Who am I?' is put with such intensity in a Shakespeare play – a question that will be given prominence again, particularly in the great tragedies. The realization that he harbours within himself those same desires for which he has sentenced Claudio directs Angelo's thoughts towards the condemned man; the self-addressed imperative virtually repeats Isabella's beseeching appeals for clemency for her brother. At the same time he also realizes that his judicial unimpeachability has been lost through his partisanship. For a moment hope is aroused in the audience that he may be willing to change his tack in time.

However, the flow of thoughts is only briefly checked. Angelo's mind reverts rapidly to Isabella, who has filled him with such powerful and unfamiliar emotions. Is it love that makes him long so ardently for another meeting? Or is it only desire? While Angelo is still interrogating his emotions, the object of his desires has already taken hold of his imagination, leading him to exclaim 'What is't I dream on?' It seems to him to be the temptation of the devil, so that he now addresses Satan as the cunning seducer who takes an angel's shape in order to lure a saint, an idea familiar to the Elizabethan audience from iconography (suggested by 2 Corinthians 11:14).

This is another allusion to Angelo's Puritanism: the Puritans were the self-styled saints of the sixteenth and seventeenth centuries. Likewise in Malvolio, Shakespeare had already exposed exaggerated self-esteem, lack of humour and the tendency to call others to order as Puritanical qualities. Angelo defines the dangerous nature of the temptation which is overwhelming him even more precisely when he says that he is tempted 'to sin in loving virtue'. Here sin is contrasted with virtue for the second time. Not only this soliloquy but the whole of the play is permeated with the language of the Bible, with Christian values. 'Judge not, that ye be not judged' is the motto of this soliloquy (see 175–6), and of the whole scene, and we will recall it several times during the course of the play.

In the last lines, spoken in a retrospective mood on the point of departure, Angelo finds his way back to a more colloquial manner of speech after the horrified exclamations of the earlier part of the soliloquy. Looking back again to his earlier mode of being and reacting, he acknowledges here once more the extent to which the meeting with Isabella has altered him. For now, he himself is 'fond' and belongs to those he used to ridicule. His self-analysis is not without a sense of irony, and not without honesty, either. Yet his attitude towards Isabella leaves no room for reciprocity or for consideration of her feelings. The thought that he could woo her honourably does not occur to him; nor does he contemplate resisting the temptation. In his next soliloquy he already has to admit to himself 'Blood, thou art blood' (II.iv.15). This finally seals his yielding to temptation.

What is it in this soliloquy that arouses the lively response of audience and reader? Not only do we experience the tremendous collapse of the inner edifice of a human being, a process which enables him to discover himself; we are ourselves involved in his dilemma. We could hardly feel warmly towards the Angelo of the opening scenes, who stood on his pedestal with icy self-assurance. Now, as he gains a certain insight into his own human fallibility and we see him before us as a tortured man racked by uncertainty, our sympathy is aroused but, like him, we are in two minds. Although he attains a higher level of self-knowledge we cannot approve the heinous attempt at emotional blackmail to which he will shortly be led. Our moral judgement is in conflict with our human sympathy. The soliloquy confronts us as well as Angelo

with questions for which we have no clear answer, arousing
in us the divided response to which Ernest Schanzer has
drawn attention in connection with this play.[18]

Cymbeline

IACHIMO IN IMOGEN'S BEDCHAMBER

II.ii.11–51

> [*Sleeps. Iachimo comes from the trunk.*]

Iachimo. The crickets sing, and man's o'er-labour'd sense
 Repairs itself by rest. Our Tarquin thus
 Did softly press the rushes, ere he waken'd
 The chastity he wounded. Cytherea,
 How bravely thou becom'st thy bed! fresh lily!   15
 And whiter than the sheets! That I might touch!
 But kiss, one kiss! Rubies unparagon'd,
 How dearly they do't: 'tis her breathing that
 Perfumes the chamber thus: the flame o' th' taper
 Bows toward her, and would under-peep her lids, 20
 To see th' enclosed lights, now canopied
 Under these windows, white and azure lac'd
 With blue of heaven's own tinct. But my design.
 To note the chamber: I will write all down:
 Such, and such pictures: there the window, such 25
 Th' adornment of her bed; the arras, figures,
 Why, such, and such; and the contents o' th' story.
 Ah, but some natural notes about her body
 Above ten thousand meaner moveables
 Would testify, t' enrich mine inventory.   30
 O sleep, thou ape of death, lie dull upon her,
 And be her sense but as a monument,
 Thus in a chapel lying. Come off, come off;
           [*Taking off her bracelet.*]
 As slippery as the Gordian knot was hard.
 'Tis mine, and this will witness outwardly,   35
 As strongly as the conscience does within,

To th' madding of her lord. On her left breast
A mole cinque-spotted: like the crimson drops
I' th' bottom of a cowslip. Here's a voucher,
Stronger than ever law could make; this secret   40
Will force him think I have pick'd the lock, and ta'en
The treasure of her honour. No more: to what end?
Why should I write this down, that's riveted,
Screw'd to my memory? She hath been reading late,
The tale of Tereus, here the leaf's turn'd down   45
Where Philomel gave up. I have enough:
To th' trunk again, and shut the spring of it.
Swift, swift, you dragons of the night, that dawning
May bare the raven's eye! I lodge in fear;
Though this a heavenly angel, hell is here.   50

                                    [Clock strikes.]

One, two, three: time, time!

                      [Goes into the trunk. The scene closes.]

Cymbeline has the largest number of soliloquies of any
Shakespeare play, and the largest number of long ones.
This does not mean that these soliloquies reach a higher
level of perfection and differentiation, for most of them are
overtly used to elucidate the very complicated plot, and to
help the audience to feel more at ease in the fairy-tale
world of romance, balancing between tragedy and
comedy. These frequent soliloquies make it impossible for
the illusion of realistic action to be sustained as it can be, for
instance, in the tragedies, but this is probably intentional
on Shakespeare's part and accepted by his audience.[19] The
experimental character of the play, resulting from the
blending of disparate genres, leads to a variety of effects
which are at times quite contrary to one another, so that
the criterion of inner consistency becomes inapplicable.
Nevertheless, in this novel manner Shakespeare succeeds
in creating effective drama and exciting situations rich in
tension. We experience moments full of vivid poetry and of

emotional intensity, which show that consistency is not the only valid criterion in the assessment of a play.

Iachimo's soliloquy in II.ii is one of those dramatic and poetic highlights which have so powerful an effect on the audience, evoking a variety of reactions.[20] This speech is remarkable in several ways: its effectiveness depends on surprise and not – as is more often the case – on careful preparation; it is also an outstanding example of a soliloquy being determined by sensory perception of the external world rather than by inner feelings, even though it may also give indirect expression to those feelings. The words of the soliloquy suggest every gesture, rendering stage directions superfluous. The audience is guided to see and absorb what Iachimo sees and recounts to himself, but at the same time the language gives free rein to the imagination, evoking, by means of classical allusions and mythological comparisons, images which transcend the action on stage.

Throughout the poetically enhanced speech the audience remains in a state of utmost suspense and expectation as to whether Iachimo's diabolical endeavour will be thwarted by Imogen's awakening. Iachimo himself is afraid of this, as he admits shortly before the end of the scene ('I lodge in fear'). The captivating beauty conveyed to us above all in the early part of the soliloquy unfolds itself against a background of a very different sort. The special quality of the scene lies in the combination of breathtaking action with the rhetoric of the language, which results in an amplifying, lingering effect.

At the beginning of the scene we see Imogen in her bedchamber; she has been reading for several hours and is now tired and ready to fall asleep ('Sleep hath seiz'd me wholly' [7]). She asks her lady to leave the taper burning by her bed, and to mark the place she has reached in the book – little details to be picked up later in Iachimo's soliloquy. Then she says her evening prayer, asking the gods to protect her 'From fairies and the tempters of the night' – in unconsciously ironical anticipation of what is to come. The lady has gone, there is silence; the stage directions read: 'Sleeps'. The audience wonders what will happen next, not knowing that Iachimo is hiding in the trunk, for, unlike Boccaccio in the source (*Decameron* II.ix), Shakespeare does not have Iachimo divulge his intention to hide in the trunk himself. We only know that Imogen has acceded readily, without the slightest suspicion, to his request that the trunk, with its valuable contents, should be placed in her bedchamber overnight for safe keeping (I.vii.180 ff). Thus the moment when the trunk opens and Iachimo climbs out has a sensational effect, startling the audience, but potentially also bordering on the comic or the grotesque, depending on the production. Whether or not the audience will already have guessed at the purpose behind this ruse of Iachimo's is open to conjecture; the terms of the wager between Iachimo and Posthumus, under which Iachimo has undertaken to prove the susceptibility of Posthumus's wife to seduction, are already known. The first twelve lines of the soliloquy, however, give no indication of what is to follow; Iachimo does not reveal his intentions immediately, and the renewed delay heightens the suspense. First of all we are attuned to the atmosphere of the well-deserved nocturnal rest, during which mankind finds repose after the fatiguing labours of the day:

> The crickets sing, and man's o'er-labour'd sense
> Repairs itself by rest.

Coming from the lips of the cynic Iachimo these lovely lines may seem surprising, but the correspondence of language and character is less important here than our recognition of the stark contrast between Imogen's untroubled sleep and the danger surrounding her. The next lines give a clearer sense of this:

> Our Tarquin thus
> Did softly press the rushes, ere he waken'd
> The chastity he wounded.

Shakespeare achieves several effects simultaneously with this one sentence: for the actor it is a direction ('thus') to step cautiously towards Imogen's bed; the words impress most clearly on the audience this stepping 'softly' (137); the allusion to the rape of Lucretia suggested by 'Our Tarquin' (12), the legendary early Roman figure, arouses a lightning awareness of the sleeping Imogen being in comparable danger.[21]

It becomes apparent after a few further lines that Iachimo's plans are following a different course. He is spellbound at the sight of the sleeping Imogen; then he addresses her (14–23). There is an inimitable interweaving of different elements in these lines. We see Iachimo's gestures and movements; while he is praising Imogen's beauty he is overcome by desire so that he approaches even closer, wishing to touch and to kiss her; he inhales the perfume of her breath, and then even includes the flame of the taper burning at the bedside in the purlieus of his wishful thinking. His eulogy of the woman he beholds is in the style of the Elizabethan lyric. Metaphorical idealization is combined with voluptuous sense perception. The ingenious comparisons and circumlocutions make the mute picture come alive; the descriptions enable us to visualize the scene.

The diction and the movement of the verse, too, contribute to the effect. Early on in the speech comes the admiring invocation of Cytherea (one of the names of Venus), with whom Iachimo identifies the sleeping Imogen. This gives way to a second address, of the 'fresh lily' (15), and the sequence closes with the comparative

device 'whiter than the sheets' (16), which takes up a
further concrete detail from the picture before us in order
to include it in the hyperbole, at the same time emphasizing Imogen's chastity. However, these lines are followed
not by the elaborate periods that would be found in the
Elizabethan lyric, but by short incomplete utterances,
broken off in mid-sentence, and accompanied by gestures,
giving the impression of simple spontaneous speech. Only
after this does the language begin to soar to poetic heights
again, elaborating on the picture that we see before us:
Imogen sleeps, her lustrous eyes are closed, the flame of the
taper would like to peep beneath her eyelids as it bows
towards the radiance that shines more brightly than it does
itself. The white skin finely veined with blue gives rise to
the unusual comparison of her eyelids with latticed
shutters. Here, as at several other points in the play,
meticulous description and close observation are fused
with ornate metaphor. It is astonishing that these eloquent
lines in praise of beauty should be spoken by Iachimo, the
villain, who is in the process of implementing a fiendish
plan against the honour of this innocent, defenceless
woman. Of course, Iachimo's vainglorious intrigue cannot
be compared with the insistent malice of a character such
as Iago; as Granville-Barker remarked, 'No tragically
potent scoundrel, we should be sure, will ever come out of a
trunk'[22]. Yet the fact that it is the Machiavellian Iachimo,
gifted with aesthetic sensibility, who opens our eyes to the
beauty of Imogen, is one of the paradoxes of the play.
Moreover, the melodious sound of the poetry of this part of
the soliloquy creates a certain distance to the action on the
stage, which is typical of this romance.

The three words 'But my design' mark the close of the
first part of the soliloquy. Iachimo announces that he is
now attending to business. His words display a sleuth's
thoroughness as he pieces together, point by point, the
irrefutable evidence of his night of love with Imogen.

Questions and interjections, self-interrogation and re-flection allow for pauses which give the actor time to linger, to gaze, to glance all round him. His eyes light on Imogen's book and he notices that she has just reached the point (in Ovid's *Metamorphoses*) where Philomel yields to the violence of Tereus. This links up with the mention of 'Our Tarquin' at the beginning of the soliloquy, throwing light on Iachimo's dark fantasies. When, with the utmost care, he lifts off her bracelet, with the twofold 'Come off, come off' and the epithet 'slippery' (for the bracelet [34; 35]), the moment is full of suspense and sensuousness, for this time the risk of Imogen's awakening is very real indeed. Not without reason does Iachimo in the two preceding lines appeal to sleep, seen here almost as his accomplice:

> O sleep, thou ape of death, lie dull upon her,
> And be her sense but as a monument,
> Thus in a chapel lying.   (31–3)

The apostrophe is suggestive of the impassioned style of the soliloquies in the tragedies, but it also matches the rhetorical pathos in Iachimo's self-dramatization, and it is an ironic anticipation of Imogen's proximity to death in the following scenes, where she only narrowly escapes the death by poison that was prepared for her.

A second apostrophe, formulated in comparable style, leads into the closing lines of the soliloquy:

> Swift, swift, you dragons of the night, that dawning
> May bare the raven's eye! I lodge in fear;
> Though this a heavenly angel, hell is here.
>   (48–50)

By these words the audience's awareness of time, held in abeyance during the soliloquy, is reawakened. At the beginning of the scene Imogen had asked the lady what time it was, and had received the answer 'Almost mid-night, madam' (2). She had asked to be woken at four o'clock in the morning. Now, at the end of the soliloquy, we are made aware that several hours have passed and it will soon be daybreak. The audience, however, will hardly realize that this contradicts the actual passage of time. The clock is already striking three, and Iachimo counts the strokes, and confirms with his final 'time, time!' that he must climb back into the trunk, thus providing a skilful transition from the soliloquy to the ensuing action of the following scene; but in the one-and-a-half lines which precede the striking of the clock there is a kind of diagram – formulated in succinct and striking terms, underscored by end-rhyme – of the strange opposition of the two people belonging to different worlds: 'heavenly angel', 'hell'. For one brief moment at the end there is a spark of moral awareness; Iachimo knows what he is doing. The sight of Imogen lying before him like an angel makes their relative positions clear to him.

This scene, which demands of the audience such attentiveness to detail and to subtlety, suggests, together with some other scenes in the play, that *Cymbeline* may have been written with a view to performance at Shakespeare's company's new private theatre at Blackfriars, where the smaller auditorium allowed a wider range of intonation and pitch, and finer nuances of feeling could be conveyed.

The Tempest

PROSPERO RENOUNCES HIS MAGIC POWER
V.i.33–57

Prospero. Ye elves of hills, brooks, standing lakes, and groves;
  And yet that on the sands with printless foot
  Do chase the ebbing Neptune, and do fly him
  When he comes back; you demi-puppets that   35
  By moonshine do the green sour ringlets make,
  Whereof the ewe not bites; and you whose pastime

Is to make midnight mushrooms, that rejoice
To hear the solemn curfew; by whose aid—   40
Weak masters though ye be—I have bedimm'd
The noontide sun, call'd forth the mutinous winds,
And 'twixt the green sea and the azur'd vault
Set roaring war: to the dread rattling thunder
Have I given fire, and rifted Jove's stout oak   45
With his own bolt; the strong-bas'd promontory
Have I made shake, and by the spurs pluck'd up
The pine and cedar: graves at my command
Have wak'd their sleepers, op'd, and let 'em forth
By my so potent Art. But this rough magic   50
I here abjure; and, when I have requir'd
Some heavenly music,—which even now I do,—
To work mine end upon their senses, that
This airy charm is for, I'll break my staff,
Bury it certain fadoms in the earth,   55
And deeper than did ever plummet sound
I'll drown my book.   *Solemn music.*

The speech in which Prospero renounces his magic art, and
thereby also his power, is the last real soliloquy that we
hear from him, for his epilogue belongs to a different
category. It is also the last scene in which Prospero appears
in his magician's attire (which he had put on for the first
time in I.ii), ceremoniously clothed in his magic robe, with
staff and book in hand. This leads the audience to expect
some decisive action. The soliloquy precedes the great
scene of forgiveness, being separated from it only by solemn
music, and the speech continues as semi-monologue after
Ariel and others have already appeared on the stage.

The soliloquy offers us some of the most evocative poetry
in the play,[23] and is very different from the earlier
soliloquies. Prospero does not turn his gaze inwards, nor
yet towards his immediate surroundings (as Iachimo does
in the soliloquy from *Cymbeline*); he contemplates the

invisible and encompasses the many-faceted phenomena of nature in such a way that the imagination of the listener opens on horizons far beyond the limits of the actual plot. In *The Tempest* we are invited several times to linger, to dwell on lyrical interludes often accompanied by music, dance or mime. With regard to the main plot these visions and meditations do not seem necessary, but they fulfil an important function in the structure of the work. They always have an indirect bearing on the inner meaning of the play, which, however, Shakespeare is careful to keep beneath the surface.[24] The efforts of the critics to grasp the essence of the play by rational means can never do justice to its special qualities, which Prospero's soliloquy exemplifies.

The way in which the action of *The Tempest* takes place throughout on two levels is more pronounced than in the other late romances. The development of the loosely constructed action, with its resolutions, agreements and plans, is often indicated in a few words or by implication only. Much more space is devoted to poetic images of nature and the supernatural. The text constantly appeals to the senses, to smell and hearing as well as sight, so that the exotic atmosphere of the island is given physical immediacy. The unreal is made real by the pervasive sense impressions, yet what is conveyed remains mysterious and often puzzling.

Our reception of Prospero's soliloquy also occurs on two levels. When he announces his resolve to give up his magic powers and part with their insignia ('I'll break my staff, / Bury it certain fadoms in the earth, / And deeper than did ever plummet sound / I'll drown my book' [54–7]), we take conscious note of this, for it speaks directly to our rational understanding. Yet these lines come towards the end of the soliloquy; the first eighteen lines have conveyed, with great intensity, something quite different. Prospero calls to mind his magic powers before he bids farewell to them; in his imagination he roves through the remotest realms of nature, indeed of the universe. A vast and variegated panorama of impressions and natural processes unfolds before our inner eye. Coleridge wrote of *The Tempest* in 1818: 'It addresses itself entirely to the imaginative faculty'.[25] Subsequently this statement, made with reference to the play as a whole, was found to apply to some parts more than to others; this soliloquy is one of those passages.

The remarkable effect of the speech is heightened by the fact that it is not prepared for, as is otherwise the case; it starts suddenly. The words which Prospero speaks before the soliloquy begins – words spoken as if to himself, although in Ariel's presence – have given no indication of inner change. When he is left alone on the stage, the audience will expect a continuation of the same train of thought, but that is not what happens; Prospero speaks as from a great height, detached from what is happening around him. In their visionary remoteness and inner loneliness his lines recall the significant words which he spoke in the preceding scene (IV.i.148), in the presence of Ferdinand and Miranda. It is worth noting that the usual criteria of characterization are not applicable to these lines, for this is a play constructed according to quite different principles.

It would be difficult to find any other passage in Shakespeare in which so many different and contrary impressions of natural phenomena are densely interwoven. What has sometimes been hinted at in the preceding acts is reinforced and supplemented here. Prospero's gaze ranges from the very small to the very large, from the almost imperceptible levity of the elves to the mighty turbulence of nature. Each line conveys new impressions to the senses. The opening line, telling us of the provenance of the elves, 'Ye elves of hills, brooks, standing lakes and groves' (33) already presents a complete landscape to us, while the two following lines transport us to the sea-shore, where the elves participate invisibly in the rising and ebbing of the tide. These 'demi-puppets' (36) have been at work in the 'sour ringlets' (37), the darker-coloured fairy rings in the grass, and in the mushrooms that shoot up overnight. The natural is joined with the supernatural, as so often in the play, and the inconspicuous with the strange. The powers stirring in the diminutive creatures can assume gigantic proportions, can be made to serve destructive and unheard-of purposes. For, as Prospero tells us, although these spirits are 'weak masters' (41), yet with their help he can darken the sun, generate lightning, thunder and wind, and even cause an earthquake. Since one extended sentence, containing a stark and rapid succession of ideas, and images, spans all this, the impact of this expansion towards the colossal cosmic dimension comes close to something superhuman, almost godlike. If Prospero has 'rifted Jove's stout oak / With his own bolt' (45–6), as he claims to have done, then this turn of phrase is more meaningful in this context than are the frequent mythological allusions in the other late plays. When he finally claims to have opened graves and wakened the dead, we do indeed receive an impression of hubris, of the impudent assumption of a power which belongs to God alone. This claim, as has often been noted, cannot be explained in terms of anything that has gone before, being entirely beyond the scope of Prospero's powers as seen and implied hitherto. For the magic accomplished by Prospero, the sage, the initiate, the wonderworker, has belonged to the realm of white magic, quite distinct from the black magic practised on the island by the witch Sycorax. In this connection it has also been pointed out that from his source, Golding's translation of Medea's conjurations from Book 7 of Ovid's *Metamorphoses*, Shakespeare took only what could be regarded as white magic, that is to say, only five of the twelve wonders, and those only in modified form; he did not draw on the evil and unnatural ones assignable to black magic. Yet we may wonder whether the terrible and destructive stirring-up of the elements which Prospero ascribes to his own power can really be regarded as white magic. Some critics have noted an inconsistency at this point, and have therefore included this part of the soliloquy among the 'disconcerting phrases' found from time to time in *The Tempest*.[26]

With the words 'my so potent art' Prospero ends his grand survey, and the emphatic phrasing stresses the great power which he has had at his command; but within the same line this is followed abruptly, in a quite different tone, by his renunciation of 'rough magic' (50),[27] formulated with the utmost brevity and finality. In Shakespeare's later plays there are few instances of so decisive and so complex a matter being expressed so emphatically in so few words – only seven words to make known a change which is of great significance for the inner and outer action of the play, and to give expression to one of its central problems. Several lines converge at this focal point.

Why does Prospero renounce his magic powers at this particular moment, when they enabled him to achieve the impossible? Why does he call them 'rough'? Several explanations spring to mind, but, as so often with Shakespeare, none is entirely satisfactory or complete. One thing that emerges from Prospero's declaration is that he has recognized his dream of founding an ideal existence with the help of magic to have been an illusion. He has also become aware of the limitations and moral ambivalence of magic; although it has made possible great achievements in material terms, there has been no improvement in the minds of men. In this connection it has also been observed that in Shakespeare's time even white magic was frowned on by the church; moreover it was often the object of scepticism in a world whose view of the cosmos was increasingly influenced by the natural sciences.[28]

Prospero's decision to abjure 'rough magic' and to sink the insignia of his power deep in the earth is accompanied by his resolve to have 'some heavenly music' (52) sound, 'To work mine end upon their senses that / This airy charm is for' (53–4). As the stage directions note, 'solemn music' sounds as soon as Prospero has spoken these words, a prelude to the appearance of the characters, still under Prospero's spell, who are led in by Ariel. Music flows mysteriously through the play, giving it a supernatural dimension, causing transformations and miracles of healing, but also bewitching 'intoxications'. Often music is at the service of Prospero and Ariel, a sensory expression of their supernatural powers. The 'heavenly music' (52) and 'solemn music' (57) help to make us aware of the profound significance of this speech of abdication, with its quality of ritual and ceremony, but it can hardly be ascribed to the 'rough magic' referred to in the same sentence; it belongs rather to a higher category of magic powers. Prospero must bid farewell to the spell-binding music also, when he enters on the new phase of his life. The power of music is demonstrated one last time in the next scene. There the transformations taking place among the nobles of Milan and their retinue are among the most spectacular in the play.

One critic has seen in the conclusion of the soliloquy 'the final resolution to harmony . . . worked out by Prospero'.[29] Others have interpreted this scene, with its musical dominance, in similar ways. However, there are insinuations of bitterness and disappointment in the continuation of the scene; the expectations aroused in the audience are not entirely fulfilled.

We should also note the secret link between Prospero's dialogue with Ariel, which immediately precedes the soliloquy, and the renunciation. Ariel had given his master an account of the pitiable condition to which Prospero's magic had reduced not only his enemies, but also Gonzalo. Prospero's reaction to this account is very important for the understanding of the soliloquy, and is therefore cited in full:

> Though with their high wrongs I am struck to
> th'quick
> Yet with my nobler reason 'gainst my fury
> Do I take part: the rarer action is
> In virtue than in vengeance: they being penitent,
> The sole drift of my purpose doth extend
> Not a frown further. Go release them, Ariel:
> My charms I'll break, their senses I'll restore,
> And they shall be themselves.   (V.i.25–32)

The change in mind and spirit that might otherwise have found expression in the soliloquy is revealed in the dialogue. A deep human emotion is touched in Prospero, he triumphs over himself, he is ready to forgive, and he forgoes the inflicting of punishment and revenge although he has been wounded to the quick by the actions of his enemies.[30] Thus his renunciation of magic can also be understood as the renunciation of the temptation to take vengeance, which magic would have enabled him to accomplish with ease. Prospero's words reveal his own awareness of the change within him, and the extent to which he feels that his task lies in a direction which will lead towards a more elevated level of human life: passion, fury and vengeance are what must be overcome in order to yield to nobler reason and virtue. This is a decisive step in Prospero's path of self-discovery, in the process of purification and recognition which he has undergone – and which does not after all lead to harmony, as the rest of the scene shows. For Prospero, endowed with superhuman wisdom and power, remains a human being who suffers, acquainted with temptation and weakness. Shortly before he finally leaves the stage we hear the words 'And my ending is despair', only, however, as part of a conditional construction.

Another point to be mentioned before we take our leave of the play is the assumption, voiced for the first time at the beginning of the last century, that with this soliloquy Shakespeare was making his own farewell to his art as dramatist and man of the theatre. Although this idea has found some support, weighty arguments against it have been brought forward.[31] It is doubtful whether it is in fact a theory open to verification. No one who makes a close study of *The Tempest* can escape the conclusion 'that it has always eluded, and may continue to elude, relevant comment'.[32]

4

Soliloquies from the tragedies

ROMEO AND JULIET
JULIUS CAESAR
HAMLET
MACBETH
OTHELLO
KING LEAR

If we want to become acquainted with Shakespeare's soliloquies at the peak of their development we must look at the soliloquies of the tragic heroes. The unfolding of the playwright's creativity is illustrated here by passages from six tragedies familiar to most readers and theatregoers. In the monologues and scenes presented in this chapter we encounter everything that is most distinctive of the art of characterization in Shakespeare's greatest plays: the illuminating compactness of expression; the portrayal of thoughts and emotions by means of forceful images appealing to the senses; the encompassing of the whole of human nature, in all its contradictory diversity. The skill with which Shakespeare integrates the soliloquies in the drama is at its most accomplished in these speeches. The dramatic quality of the soliloquies, which has been referred to several times, is enhanced; many ways of including an element of dialogue in the monologue are found, providing new and unusual forms of interlocution. In *Antony and Cleopatra*, *Coriolanus* and *Timon of Athens* we find examples of further functions and uses of the soliloquy. These speeches, however, do not have the weight or the significance of those included in this chapter; for this reason, and because of limitations of space, they are not dealt with in our study.

Romeo and Juliet

The lovers' soliloquies in *Romeo and Juliet* may be seen as the acme of Shakespeare's art in the early period, which extends up to the middle of the fifteen-nineties. These soliloquies are an integral part of the situation in which they arise; the spoken word conveys to us not only the setting but also the alternation of day and night, of light and shade, and we are made strongly aware of the passage of time. The soliloquies occur at key points in the dramatic rhythm of the play, deepening our sympathetic involvement in the destiny and the personality of the speakers. Two of the four speeches chosen for discussion belong to the first half of the play and are rooted in a situation in which, in the consciousness of the lovers, love's happiness is not yet threatened by the tragic chain of events of the last two acts, from which the two further soliloquies are taken.

ROMEO'S NOCTURNAL SOLILOQUY IN THE ORCHARD
II.ii.1–25

[*Romeo comes forward.*]

Romeo. He jests at scars that never felt a wound.
        [*Enter* JULIET *above.*]
But soft, what light through yonder window breaks?
It is the east and Juliet is the sun!
Arise fair sun and kill the envious moon
Who is already sick and pale with grief   5
That thou her maid art far more fair than she.
Be not her maid since she is envious,
Her vestal livery is but sick and green
And none but fools do wear it. Cast it off.
It is my lady, O it is my love!
O that she knew she were!   10
She speaks, yet she says nothing. What of that?
Her eye discourses, I will answer it.
I am too bold. 'Tis not to me she speaks.
Two of the fairest stars in all the heaven,   15
Having some business, do entreat her eyes
To twinkle in their spheres till they return.
What if her eyes were there, they in her head?
The brightness of her cheek would shame those stars
As daylight doth a lamp. Her eyes in heaven   20
Would through the airy region stream so bright
That birds would sing and think it were not night.
See how she leans her cheek upon her hand.
O that I were a glove upon that hand,
That I might touch that cheek.

Romeo's first great soliloquy[1] follows on directly from the mockingly witty words which Mercutio and Benvolio have exchanged on the subject of his love-sickness. At the beginning of the previous scene, which leads into the orchard scene without a break (II.ii), Romeo had stolen away over the garden wall;[2] from his hiding place in the background, quite noticeable to the audience, he has been listening to these drastic and bawdy remarks with their stark reference to himself. It is hardly possible to imagine a stronger contrast to the emotions which have filled him since his first meeting with Juliet, but Mercutio, the mocking cynic, who speaks so coarsely, has no idea of the change wrought in Romeo. He thinks that his friend is in love with Rosaline; his words aim to show up the sentimental infatuation presented to us in the first scene of the play, but now they are wide of the mark. With a single sentence Romeo refutes Mercutio's imputation and makes clear to us the altered condition of his own spirit: 'He jests at scars that never felt a wound' (1).

Romeo utters this short sentence after the departure of Mercutio and Benvolio, as he comes forward onto the platform and all attention is directed towards him. This demonstrates Shakespeare's skill in bringing about a transition between contrasting emotions, which is sudden and yet not abrupt. These few words are sufficient to cause the mood to swing right round: the word 'wound' puts us on the alert; Mercutio's lewd jokes lose all immediacy. Yet these very jokes have their importance, emphasizing what follows by contrast.

Romeo's second sentence is no less revealing. He looks up to where Juliet appears above at a lighted window; our gaze follows his. On several further occasions in this speech Romeo draws us into his visual or imaginary experience. Because of this we may not even realize with what precision the scene is set from the start of the speech, with indication of staging and positioning of the characters, but as is frequently the case with Shakespeare, externals are soon transfigured and, in the course of the soliloquy, give cosmic dimensions.[3] The setting itself is symbolic: Romeo stands below in the garden, separated from Juliet, to whom his gaze and his longing ascend – a separation striving towards union.

The soliloquy moves between two poles; poetic similes and metaphors alternate with direct address and renewed perception of concrete detail. Staccato diction ('She speaks, yet she says nothing; what of that?' [12]) gives way to enraptured hyperbole. The silent presence of the beloved, whose every move he observes, anchors the soliloquy in the here and now, preventing it from becoming diffused in remote abstraction. As our imagination is drawn into his upward gaze, for us, too, Juliet, appearing at the window above, may seem transfigured.

The opening comparison of Juliet with the sun (3–9), which is to 'kill the envious moon' sounds fanciful and artificial to our ears. Here a motif employed by the Elizabethan sonneteers, and thoroughly familiar to Shakespeare's audience, is used to give expression not only to lyric adoration of the beloved but also to the impetuous yearning of the lover. The envious moon, equated with the chaste goddess Diana, is to be eliminated so that Juliet, the sun, can give herself to Romeo wholly and unreservedly. These lines, rich in allusions, end with the brusque imperative concerning virginity: 'Cast it off'. Such a transition from elaborate rhetoric to colloquial straightforwardness is typical of the style and structure of the play as a whole.

The next five lines are without poetic adornment. In the rapid sequence of exclamations, questions and observations Romeo's upward gaze is linked with self-interrogation, discovery, desire and resolve. This is succeeded at once by a cosmic vision in which the light of the stars is exchanged for Juliet's shining eyes. The image is extended still further: the brightness radiating from Juliet's cheeks and eyes would make the starlight seem dim, like a

lamp compared with bright daylight; it would so transform
the night that the birds, thinking it was day, would start to
sing. These lines have two effects: Juliet at her window is
integrated in the nocturnal landscape of the imagination
with the starry sky and clouds; at the same time there is the
imagery of light, a dominant leitmotif in the play, giving
expression to the passion of the lovers.[4] The rhyming
of two key words ('bright': 'night') makes us particularly
attentive to the symbolism of light and dark. Moreover, if
we read the lines aloud we notice how the soliloquy
approaches this climax with a gradual crescendo. The
sequence of vowel sounds, extended sentence structures,
metrical patterns and tempo combine to express the
ecstasy that has taken hold of Romeo's imagination at this
point. Yet only for a moment. In the next line he is gazing
again at the figure at the window above ('See how she leans
her cheek upon her hand' [23]). This time visual perception is not transposed into far-reaching fantasy, but into a
longing for physical closeness (24-5). Yet only two lines
further on – after the two words uttered by Juliet – we
return to the transfiguration of the beloved. In these lines
the firmament with its luminaries is vividly evoked. As
before, moon and stars are not mere metaphors, but help to
conjure up the nocturnal setting – the dark garden above
which clouds move slowly in a starlit sky.

Our passage ends just before Juliet's first 'Ay me!'. These
words are not addressed to Romeo, whom she has not yet
noticed in the garden below. Thus they are in the nature of
a soliloquy, as are the following lines 33-6. The actual
dialogue does not develop until later. Shakespeare creates
a speech situation bordering on soliloquy which has a
particular impact on the audience because the lovers are
together yet separate, and addressing their thoughts to one
another. We look forward to the moment when the
genuine dialogue will begin. The transition from monologue to dialogue, broached here so gradually, signifies the

overcoming of separation. The symbolism of the tableau is mirrored in the speech situation.

JULIET LONGS FOR HER WEDDING NIGHT
III.ii.1–31

Enter JULIET *alone.*

Juliet. Gallop apace, you fiery-footed steeds,
   Towards Phoebus' lodging. Such a waggoner
   As Phaeton would whip you to the west
   And bring in cloudy night immediately.
   Spread thy close curtain, love-performing night,   5
   That runaway's eyes may wink, and Romeo
   Leap to these arms untalk'd-of and unseen.
   Lovers can see to do their amorous rites
   By their own beauties; or, if love be blind,
   It best agrees with night. Come, civil night,   10
   Thou sober-suited matron, all in black,
   And learn me how to lose a winning match
   Play'd for a pair of stainless maidenhoods.
   Hood my unmann'd blood, bating in my cheeks,
   With thy black mantle, till strange love grow bold,   15
   Think true love acted simple modesty.
   Come night, come Romeo, come thou day in night,
   For thou wilt lie upon the wings of night
   Whiter than new snow upon a raven's back.
   Come gentle night, come loving black-brow'd night, 20
   Give me my Romeo; and when I shall die
   Take him and cut him out in little stars,
   And he will make the face of heaven so fine
   That all the world will be in love with night,
   And pay no worship to the garish sun.   25
   O, I have bought the mansion of a love
   But not possess'd it, and though I am sold,
   Not yet enjoy'd. So tedious is this day
   As is the night before some festival
   To an impatient child that hath new robes   30
   And may not wear them.

Juliet's great soliloquy invites comparison with Romeo's soliloquy (II.ii). Both speeches are rich in poetry, with a remarkable blending of elaborately rhetorical language and directness of expression; in both the imagery encompasses not only the night and the cosmos with its galaxies, but also the obvious and the close-at-hand[5]; in both there is close involvement with the beings and powers addressed – alternately with the beloved and the numinous in nature – but Romeo had been soliloquizing to his beloved at the window above, whereas Juliet believes herself to be alone, and her aloneness – and anticipation of being united with her lover – contributes to the atmosphere and tone of the soliloquy.

Several elements of Juliet's soliloquy, however, are new and different. Its effect depends largely on the audience being aware of something which she does not yet know, although she is to hear it later on in the same scene. There are ample echoes of the Elizabethan lyric, and the soliloquy reflects the set patterns of the literary genre 'epithalamium' (nuptial song) handed down from classical antiquity. However, the sense of the passage of time is new; time passes in this case too slowly as Juliet waits impatiently for night. Thus the audience is given a clear awareness of the specific dramatic rhythm of the play.

The immediately preceding scene (III.i) was the eventful one in which Mercutio and Tybalt met their deaths and Romeo was banished, a prelude to the tragic doom of the two lovers. While Escalus' last inexorable words 'Mercy but murders, pardoning those who kill' still ring in our ears, Juliet knows nothing of these events, and this adds a tragic undertone to her soliloquy.[6] She still hopes for the consummation of the great love which, as *we* know, is threatened with disaster. Some of her words, in particular the lines foreshadowing the shared death to which love will lead (21–5), have a greater significance than she imagines.

The soliloquy begins with a formal apostrophe, with

mythological images and allusions which would have been familiar to an Elizabethan audience. Yet there is an amazing contrast between this richly ornamented speech of Juliet's and her mode of expression in the early scenes. Shakespeare has Juliet speak her own epithalamium in anticipation of her wedding night. The forms and themes of this literary genre, which had been revived by Shakespeare's contemporaries (Sidney, Spenser and others), are ironically inverted and set, as it were, in a different key. Prothalamium and epithalamium were part of the ritual celebration of a marriage, offered to the bridal pair by a poet, an allegorical figure, a chorus, but not spoken by the bride herself. But for Juliet there can be no public celebration (5–7). That she must speak her own epithalamium emphasizes her aloneness, the need for secrecy to which both she and Romeo must submit.

Juliet's impatience finds unconventional expression in the very first lines of the speech. Not only does she spur on the sun god's steeds, so that night may draw in sooner, she also longs for Phaeton to be waggoner so that the sun may sink even faster. Phaeton was allowed to drive his father Apollo's sun chariot for one day, and through his haste he precipitated a great disaster. The Elizabethans knew this story well in Golding's translation of Ovid's *Metamorphoses*; the mention of Phaeton at this point would have been understood as a veiled hint of impending doom.

That a girl of not yet fourteen years of age should speak these allusive lines may seem strange to us, but only for a moment, because after the first four lines this gives way to another impression. Juliet, inexperienced as she is, tells openly and directly of her longing for the wedding night, and she invokes the night as her ally to grant her protection and darkness. No one is to know, no one is to see. Cupid, the god of love (implied in all probability by 'runaway'),[7] shall also close his eyes, while to Juliet herself the night will bring courage and safety. The imagery derived from

falconry is part of the verbal artifice of courtly love, a
means of avoiding direct expression. It is as if Shakespeare
himself would like to draw a protective veil over the events
of this night, which Juliet refers to in terms of sensuous
purity: 'Think true love acted simple modesty'. In Victorian times this first part of the soliloquy was often cut
because it was felt to be indecorous.[8] That has changed; we
in the meantime are moved by the simple honesty, indeed
innocence, of Juliet's passionate affirmation in all its
youthfulness.

The question arises as to the effect in this context of the
elaborately rhetorical form and wording of the soliloquy.
Five times night is invoked and appealed to for assistance;
the increasingly insistent imperative forms (more than a
dozen of them, half of them 'Come') recurring throughout
the soliloquy, underline the mood of impatience and
heartfelt longing, repeatedly giving the monologue the
tone of a dialogue. Night appears each time in a different
guise, as 'love-performing night' (5), as 'civil night' (10)
and 'sober-suited matron' (11), as 'gentle night' and
'loving black-brow'd night' (20). The notions that Juliet
associates with the night stem from the protected existence
of her childhood, notwithstanding the extent to which she
is already accepting her own destiny, as demonstrated by
this soliloquy and by the scene that follows it. With these
appellations Juliet is projecting her own hopes and desires
onto the night, but at the same time the night is to be
intermediary and assistance for Romeo as well.

Thus – in the second half of the soliloquy – the simple
transposition 'Come, night, come, Romeo . . .' can take
place. But this simplicity again proves to be the starting-
point for a great sweep of imagination, taking the gaze
away from the earth and up to heaven. As Romeo in his
soliloquy (II.ii) beheld his beloved transfigured in radiance, so also Juliet envisages a figurative sequence based
on the same contrast of light and dark (day and night),

although her images are closer to nature and to the senses than those used by Romeo. The subsequent vision of the future, transposing the beloved after her death (a tragic presentiment) to the firmament and transforming him into little stars that shine there, combines cosmic dimensions with childhood imagination. The last lines, bringing us back to the immediate present, in which Juliet compares her impatience with that of a child who has been given new clothes and may not yet wear them (30–1), remind us once again that we are listening to a girl who has not yet outgrown her childhood emotions. This duality of simplicity and childhood on the one hand and courage and maturity on the other makes the soliloquy particularly moving.

The question arises as to why Shakespeare gave to the soliloquy this particular kind of language, distinctly reminiscent of the Elizabethan lyric. The well-wrought poetry spoken by Romeo and Juliet, with its musicality and evocative imagery, elevates the lovers above the level of the other characters, and adds a further dimension to their soliloquies. At the same time it arouses the sympathy of the audience. The great hymn of love, the panegyric which is the central theme of this play, needs to be celebrated by exceptional language, so that the great happiness of the lovers' meeting in all its radiant transience may be impressed indelibly on our minds. The sonnet form of the lines spoken by Romeo and Juliet on the occasion of their first encounter at the masked ball serves this purpose,[9] as do the hymnic lines of transfiguration in Romeo's soliloquy (II.ii). The elevated style alerts us to the fact that something out of the ordinary is happening; but each time there is a return to natural spontaneity. We feel the trust and intimacy of the lovers all the more closely after the distancing effect of the conventions and allusions. The transition from one style to the other is often, as in this soliloquy, almost imperceptible.

JULIET RESOLVES TO DRINK THE POTION
IV.iii.12–58

Lady Capulet.   Good night.
  Get thee to bed and rest, for thou hast need.
                              Exeunt [Lady Capulet and Nurse].
Juliet. Farewell. God knows when we shall meet again.   15
    I have a faint cold fear thrills through my veins
    That almost freezes up the heat of life.
    I'll call them back again to comfort me.
    —Nurse!—What should she do here?
    My dismal scene I needs must act alone.
    Come, vial.   20
    What if this mixture do not work at all?
    Shall I be married then tomorrow morning?
    No! No! This shall forbid it. Lie thou there.
                              [She lays down a knife.]
    What if it be a poison which the Friar
    Subtly hath minister'd to have me dead,   25
    Lest in this marriage he should be dishonour'd,
    Because he married me before to Romeo?
    I fear it is. And yet methinks it should not,
    For he hath still been tried a holy man.
    How if, when I am laid into the tomb,   30
    I wake before the time that Romeo
    Come to redeem me? There's a fearful point!
    Shall I not then be stifled in the vault,
    To whose foul mouth no healthsome air breathes in,
    And there die strangled ere my Romeo comes?   35
    Or, if I live, is it not very like,
    The horrible conceit of death and night
    Together with the terror of the place,
    As in a vault, an ancient receptacle
    Where for this many hundred years the bones   40
    Of all my buried ancestors are pack'd,
    Where bloody Tybalt yet but green in earth

Lies festering in his shroud; where, as they say,
At some hours in the night spirits resort—
Alack, alack! Is it not like that I
So early waking, what with loathsome smells,   45
And shrieks like mandrakes torn out of the earth,
That living mortals, hearing them, run mad—
O, if I wake, shall I not be distraught,
Environed with all these hideous fears,
And madly play with my forefathers' joints,   50
And pluck the mangled Tybalt from his shroud,
And, in this rage, with some great kinsman's bone
As with a club dash out my desperate brains?
O look, methinks I see my cousin's ghost
Seeking out Romeo that did spit his body   55
Upon a rapier's point! Stay, Tybalt, stay!
Romeo, Romeo, Romeo, here's drink! I drink to thee!
                          She falls upon her bed within the curtains.

Between Juliet's soliloquy in III.ii, spoken at the height of
love's happiness, and the soliloquy in IV.iii, a great change
has taken place. Since the lovers' farewell in the last scene
of Act III it is Juliet who has aroused the greatest
sympathy. The burdens laid on her in one situation after
another – of strain, of enforced dissimulation, of increasing
isolation – are of enormous proportions. In bold defiance of
her own fears she consents to follow a desperate path,
leading into darkness and uncertainty. In order to evade
the arranged marriage with Paris she resolves, on the
advice of Friar Laurence, to feign death by means of a
potion that will deaden all the senses. In a most concentrated form we experience the ripening of her resolve.
Shakespeare's dramatic art makes it seem so credible that
we do not question the psychological probability of so
speedy a development,[10] which we have already begun to
observe in the preceding scenes. Up to now we have only
been able to guess at the exact nature of her inner conflict,

but now she reveals it all. We see her being torn between resolve and doubt. Her dilemma is expressed not only in words: the art of the soliloquy is manifested here in the interplay of movement, properties and setting. The monologue becomes an increasingly dramatic scene, with the action taking place on several levels, anticipating towards the end of the scene the ultimate events of the play. As is so often the case at focal points of a Shakespeare play, past, present and future are interwoven, as are reality and fantasy.

Shakespeare has made careful preparations for this monologue scene. Juliet has said several times that she wants to be left alone (IV.iii. 2 and 79), so that we are expecting this situation to arise. From Friar Laurence we have already heard a precise description of the apparent death (IV.i.95 ff), and we know that Juliet must reach her decision this very night. The imagery has darkened; it is no longer pervaded by beauty and radiance, but by premonitions of death. We hear of tomb and vault, of wild beasts and suicide. By means of ironic contrast the opening of the scene, between Juliet and the nurse, also provides effective preparation for the soliloquy: they are looking out the best clothes for the wedding ('Ay, those attires are best' [1]). Then Lady Capulet sends her child to bed, wishing her a good night's rest.

Juliet describes the state both of her body and of her mind at the beginning of the soliloquy, expressing her premonitions, after she has called goodbye to her mother and the nurse, that she will never see them again. At many points in the play there are concrete indications of the appearance of the main characters; their appearance matches their state of mind and spirit. There is a high degree of awareness behind the description which Juliet gives of herself in lines 15 and 16, and also in the statement 'My dismal scene I needs must act alone' (19). There is more in this than the metaphor of playacting which we encounter so often in Shakespeare – more also than the explanatory function of the soliloquy which Shakespeare derived from early Elizabethan tragedy and used above all in his early plays. In the desperate situation in which Juliet now finds herself, these lines, prelude to an 'acted' soliloquy, have the ring of conviction.

Juliet's epithalamium was clearly structured, with its co-ordinated sequence of invocations and appeals, variations on a single theme; but here the situation is entirely different. The verse form, determined by inner turmoil, is close to prose; questions, exclamations, brief statements are punctuated by pauses. The thoughts do not, as in the earlier soliloquy, tend in one direction; doubts and fears rise to the surface, in conflict with the decisions that are trying to overcome them. In line 36 a long sentence begins, starting with a question, into which more and more adverbial clauses are inserted (40, 42, 43). In these Juliet's dreadful memories and anxieties are articulated, until the sentence is suddenly broken off so that after nine lines the initial question 'Is it not like that I . . .' has to be repeated (45). The entangled sentence structure mirrors Juliet's confusion, her succumbing to premonitions of the tomb. Thus the soliloquy conveys to us a sense not only of the here and now, but also of the future, with one giving way to the other as Juliet's contradictory emotions and anxieties are translated into action.

Many themes are touched on in these forty lines: Juliet's decision to call back her mother and the nurse ('to comfort me') is revoked; she takes the vial (20); the uneasy question of whether the drink will take effect (21) leads to her decision to have a dagger at hand in the event of marriage being forced upon her; she lays her dagger by her side (23). What if the drink should prove lethal, and Friar Laurence should have deceived her (24–6)? These doubts, however, are swiftly countered (28). But then a new fear arises, a fear of waking in the vault before Romeo appears (30–2). The vault takes shape before her inner eye; she knows it, since for centuries her ancestors have been laid to rest there (41). New questions press upon her: will she wake too soon and suffocate in the vault (43), or will the horror of the place make her lose her senses (49)? Already this seems a possibility; the idea expands to a macabre vision in which Juliet sees herself 'distraught' (49), madly playing with her forefathers' joints (51), and tugging the bloody Tybalt from his shroud. Swift as lightning the horrifying fantasy of things to come merges with hallucination as she sees Tybalt's ghost rise up before her to seek out Romeo and wreak vengeance upon him. The hallucination takes hold of her entirely. She wants to hold Tybalt back in order to protect Romeo: 'Stay, Tybalt, stay!' And three times she cries 'Romeo!' With this despairing and imploring cry, in which lie all her hopes and fears, she calls herself back to reality, and grasps the vial for the second time; this time she empties it and sinks down onto her bed to her apparent death. The transition from the drama of the waking dream to the drama of the external action is achieved almost without our noticing it; it seems natural and inevitable. The inner conflict and the enacted scene are over. The drinking of the potion is presented to us as an act of outstanding courage and extraordinary willpower, because Shakespeare has revealed to us so clearly the deep distress that went before it. Juliet's last great soliloquy convinces us that she can be called a 'tragic heroine'. Her isolation in this dramatic situation is indicative of her tragedy; after Romeo's banishment and her dismissal of the nurse she is allowed no further dialogue – not even, strictly speaking, in her last words to Romeo.

ROMEO ENTERS THE TOMB

V.iii.72–120

Paris. O, I am slain! If thou be merciful,
Open the tomb, lay me with Juliet.   [*Paris dies.*]

Romeo. In faith I will. Let me peruse this face.
Mercutio's kinsman, noble County Paris!   75
What said my man, when my betossed soul
Did not attend him, as we rode? I think
He told me Paris should have married Juliet.
Said he not so? Or did I dream it so?
Or am I mad, hearing him talk of Juliet,   80
To think it was so? O, give me thy hand,
One writ with me in sour misfortune's book.
I'll bury thee in a triumphant grave.
A grave? O no, a lantern, slaughter'd youth.
For here lies Juliet, and her beauty makes   85
This vault a feasting presence, full of light.
Death, lie thou there, by a dead man interr'd.
How oft when men are at the point of death
Have they been merry! Which their keepers call
A lightning before death. O how may I   90
Call this a lightning? O my love, my wife,
Death that hath suck'd the honey of thy breath
Hath had no power yet upon thy beauty.
Thou art not conquer'd. Beauty's ensign yet
Is crimson in thy lips and in thy cheeks,   95
And Death's pale flag is not advanced there.
Tybalt, liest thou there in thy bloody sheet?
O, what more favour can I do to thee
Than with that hand that cut thy youth in twain
To sunder his that was thine enemy?   100
Forgive me, cousin. Ah, dear Juliet,
Why art thou yet so fair? Shall I believe
That unsubstantial Death is amorous,
And that the lean abhorred monster keeps
Thee here in dark to be his paramour?   105
For fear of that I still will stay with thee,
And never from this palace of dim night
Depart again. Here, here, will I remain
With worms that are thy chambermaids. O here

Will I set up my everlasting rest   110
And shake the yoke of inauspicious stars
From this world-wearied flesh. Eyes, look your last.
Arms, take your last embrace! And lips, O you
The doors of breath, seal with a righteous kiss
A dateless bargain to engrossing Death.   115
Come, bitter conduct, come unsavoury guide,
Thou desperate pilot now at once run on
The dashing rocks thy seasick weary bark.
Here's to my love! [*He drinks.*] O true apothecary,
Thy drugs are quick. Thus with a kiss I die.   120
                                                            [*He*] *falls.*

Romeo's last soliloquy and Juliet's last soliloquy also invite
comparison, as did the two earlier ones. In both of them
there is an inner development leading to the drinking of the
potion or the poisonous drug; in drinking each lover thinks
devotedly of the other. Each soliloquy gives a last portrait
gathering all the threads together, clarifying the changes
that have been wrought, causing us to cast our minds back
in spite of the moving events presented on stage. Both
soliloquies are close to death, filled with images of
transience and dying. The vault, with the horrors that
Juliet had anticipated in her imagination (IV.iii.33 ff;
IV.iii.39 ff), is now the actual setting for the action.
Already in the first part of the scene the graveyard
atmosphere is powerfully evoked by the language, but
Romeo's soliloquy adds to this, drawing our attention to
the symbolic quality of the vault as the setting of the final
scene.[11] It conveys to us most powerfully the sombreness of
the place and the symbolism of light and dark which also
pervaded the first two soliloquies.[12] Romeo forces the tomb
open, sees Juliet, and says: 'her beauty makes / This vault a
feasting presence full of light' (85–6). Again, both soliloquies provide examples of transition from one style to
another, and of the dovetailing of inner and outer action.

Romeo's soliloquy unfolds step by step in accordance with what he finds and notices on stage.[13] Almost every sentence in the soliloquy, and the accompanying action, arise from these discoveries and observations; at the same time there is a sudden strengthening of the will, a recollection, a calling in question or a reflection (76 ff, 84, 88, 90). To an even greater degree than the soliloquies examined so far, this one is 'performed'. We can infer the sequence of movements from the text, can see how Romeo bends towards Paris, whom he only now recognizes, takes his hand, drags him towards the tomb and opens it. We see how his eyes light on Juliet, how he embraces her and kisses her, empties the vial, kisses her one last time, and dies.

Yet this listing gives only the skeleton of the action; it does not convey the shape and movement of the verse, in which tempo and diction are adapted to each moment and its specific content: lingering and restrained when Juliet's beauty, as yet undimmed by death, is described, as in line 94 ('Beauty's ensign . . .'), painfully questioning or challenging, working to a resolve (118) or expressing a sudden insight, as in the brief questions, commands and exclamations (112 ff, 119). Ceremonious gravity and formal address, as in the richly allusive lines directed to the vial, 'Come, bitter conduct . . .', or stylized metaphors of death reminiscent of the diction of Elizabethan sonnets (96, 104) are juxtaposed with tender devotion (91, 101) expressed in unpretentious terms, or with straightforward pragmatic phrasing: 'Here's to my love' (119). The extremes of death and love are closely interwoven.

A wide range of sentence structures and attitudes unfolds, in keeping with the mixture of lyricism and prosaic language which is a recurrent characteristic of this play. Even a more detailed analysis of structure, beyond the scope of this study, would not do justice to the unique effect of this soliloquy. The musical rhythm of the verse, the finely nuanced variations of sound in the sequence of phrases and sentences, can make us aware of something that is hardly susceptible of critical analysis. We sense that a different Romeo is speaking to us here, that the youth has become a man to whom the presentiment of approaching death brings neither wild despair nor frenzy, but deep seriousness, even equanimity. There is something here of the remoteness of the man who has settled his account with life and has thus achieved insight which would not have been accessible to him before ('How oft when men are at the point of death / Have they been merry!' [88–9]). This gives added poignancy to his repeated farewells, as he gazes at Juliet, still so close to life. The tenderness with which Romeo describes everything he sees is all the more devastating and tragically ironic because we know just how close his questioning is to the truth. We may yet harbour secret hopes that Juliet will now wake, for the moment of her awakening is imminent. We also wait impatiently for the arrival of Friar Laurence, fearing at the same time, however, that the watchmen may come and discover Romeo. This dual expectation arouses in the audience a tense awareness of the rapid passage of time; very soon an irrevocable end will come. This oppressive sense of time is very different from the absorption with which Romeo gazes at Juliet, oblivious of everything else around him. With his awareness of the proximity of death ('A lightning before death' [90]), he steps outside the course of events, into timelessness. The moving impact of the soliloquy is partially brought about by this disparity between Romeo's reactions and those of the audience.

Looking back to Juliet's soliloquy before her drinking of the potion we also see a great difference between her stance and his, quite contrary to the situation in the early part of the play. Romeo was at first exalted and extravagant, but now he speaks with measured gravity, conscious of 'misfortune' (82) and the 'inauspicious stars' (111), whose yoke he will now cast off, accepting death as his inescapable destiny. Juliet, on the other hand, who in the first part of the tragedy spoke with greater restraint and common sense, is driven to the utmost despair, and, through the excesses of the imagination, close to the brink of madness.

Julius Caesar

BRUTUS TORN BY INNER CONFLICT
II.i. 1–85

Enter BRUTUS *in his Orchard.*

Bru. What, Lucius, ho!
  I cannot, by the progress of the stars,
  Give guess how near to day. Lucius, I say!
  I would it were my fault to sleep so soundly.
  When, Lucius, when? Awake, I say! What, Lucius!   5

Enter LUCIUS.

Luc. Call'd you, my lord?
Bru. Get me a taper in my study, Lucius:
  When it is lighted, come and call me here.
Luc. I will, my lord.   [*Exit.*
Bru. It must be by his death: and for my part,   10
  I know no personal cause to spurn at him,
  But for the general. He would be crown'd:
  How that might change his nature, there's the question.
  It is the bright day that brings forth the adder,
  And that craves wary walking. Crown him?—that;—15
  And then, I grant, we put a sting in him,
  That at his will he may do danger with.
  Th' abuse of greatness is when it disjoins
  Remorse from power; and, to speak truth of Caesar,
  I have not known when his affections sway'd   20
  More than his reason. But 'tis a common proof,
  That lowliness is young ambition's ladder,

Whereto the climber-upward turns his face;
But when he once attains the upmost round,
He then unto the ladder turns his back,   25
Looks in the clouds, scorning the base degrees
By which he did ascend. So Caesar may;
Then lest he may, prevent. And since the quarrel
Will bear no colour for the thing he is,
Fashion it thus: that what he is, augmented,   30
Would run to these and these extremities;
And therefore think him as a serpent's egg,
Which, hatch'd, would, as his kind, grow mischievous,
And kill him in the shell.

Enter LUCIUS.

Luc. The taper burneth in your closet, sir.   35
    Searching the window for a flint, I found
    This paper, thus seal'd up; and I am sure
    It did not lie there when I went to bed.
                                [Gives him the letter.
Bru. Get you to bed again; it is not day.
    Is not to-morrow, boy, the ides of March?   40
Luc. I know not, sir.
Bru. Look in the calendar, and bring me word.
Luc. I will, sir.   *[Exit.]*
Bru. The exhalations whizzing in the air
    Give so much light that I may read by them.   45
                    [Opens the letter, and reads.]
    Brutus, thou sleep'st; awake, and see thyself.
    Shall Rome, etc. Speak, strike, redress!
    "Brutus, thou sleep'st; awake!"
    Such instigations have been often dropp'd
    Where I have took them up.   50
    "Shall Rome, etc." Thus must I piece it out:
    Shall Rome stand under one man's awe? What,
    Rome?

My ancestors did from the streets of Rome
The Tarquin drive, when he was call'd a king.
"Speak, strike, redress!" Am I entreated   55
To speak, and strike? O Rome, I make thee promise,
If the redress will follow, thou receivest
Thy full petition at the hand of Brutus.

Enter LUCIUS.

Luc. Sir, March is wasted fifteen days.   [*Knock within.*]
Bru. 'Tis good. Go to the gate; somebody knocks.   60
                                                    [*Exit Lucius.*]
Since Cassius first did whet me against Caesar,
I have not slept.
Between the acting of a dreadful thing
And the first motion, all the interim is
Like a phantasma, or a hideous dream: 65
The genius and the mortal instruments
Are then in council; and the state of man,
Like to a little kingdom, suffers then
The nature of an insurrection.

Enter LUCIUS.

Luc. Sir, 'tis your brother Cassius at the door,   70
    Who doth desire to see you.
Bru.   Is he alone?
Luc. No, sir, there are moe with him.
Bru.   Do you know them?
Luc. No, sir, their hats are pluck'd about their ears,
    And half their faces buried in their cloaks,
    That by no means I may discover them   75
    By any mark of favour.
Bru.   Let 'em enter.   [*Exit Lucius.*]
    They are the faction. O conspiracy,
Sham'st thou to show thy dangerous brow by night,
When evils are most free? O, then by day

Where wilt thou find a cavern dark enough   80
To mask thy monstrous visage? Seek none, conspiracy;
Hide it in smiles and affability:
For if thou path, thy native semblance on,
Not Erebus itself were dim enough
To hide thee from prevention.   85

Here, as in the second part of *Henry IV* (III.i) the loneliness
of the night prompts a man oppressed by cares and
burdened by great responsibilities to give vent to his
thoughts and feelings in a soliloquy; but here Shakespeare
chooses a different means of achieving complexity. Three
times Brutus is interrupted in his soliloquy by the boy
Lucius, thus three times the soliloquy can take a new
course, showing us a different aspect of his character and
influencing our attitude towards him. Lucius, who is not
mentioned in the source, Plutarch's *Lives*, seems to have
been created by Shakespeare for the express purpose of
fulfilling an important function in this situation (and in an
analogous one in IV.iii).[14] At the beginning of the scene
and again (229) towards the end we see him sound asleep,
offsetting the sleeplessness of his master, who himself draws
our attention to this contrast at the beginning and in the
middle of the soliloquy sequence (4, 62). When Brutus
speaks to Lucius, who is still very much a child, there is a
tone of affectionate care and kindness in his words which
modifies our impression of him as remote, brooding and
preoccupied, making him a more sympathetic character.

Between the exits and entrances of Lucius, intervals of
solitude arise in which it seems natural for the soliloquy to
develop. At the beginning of the scene the boy is roused
and sent to light a taper in the study. When he returns he
brings with him a sealed letter which he has found on the
window-sill, and is given a new task: to look in the calendar
and see whether the next day is the Ides of March. A little
later, after Brutus has opened the letter and read it, Lucius

confirms the fateful date, the significance of which has been imprinted on our minds in the first act. There are further moments for Brutus to be alone on the stage when Lucius is twice sent out to answer a knock at the door.

The particular effect of this soliloquy sequence is achieved not only by means of the spoken text but also by the skilfully contrived details of the setting. At the very beginning a few words evoke the location, the time of night and the atmosphere.[15] 'Enter Brutus in his orchard' may well be one of the stage directions which can be attributed to Shakespeare himself. There is a symbolic significance in the orchard, for it is part of a secluded and idyllic garden, an exclusively private place contrasting with the street, the setting of the previous dramatic scene. When Brutus later remarks on the 'exhalations' caused by meteors, this signifies the intrusion of the outside world; it is followed by the actual intrusion of the conspirators who enter at the end of the scene. Brutus is not allowed any seclusion, he may not stand aloof. As in *Romeo and Juliet* our attention is directed not only towards the language but also towards the stage business accompanying the inner change in Brutus. We sense that time is passing, and are eager to see what will come next, although the soliloquy repeatedly carries us away from the present to a great distance, and also into the depths of Brutus's mind.

Lucius's interruptions also make us aware of how preoccupied Brutus is with his own conflicts. Reflection regains the upper hand as soon as he is alone again. His absorption is further emphasized by the fact that he seems quite unmoved by the terrible nocturnal storm that dominated the previous scene. Brutus's first soliloquy allows myriad interpretations of his character.[16] Coleridge was one of the first critics unable to produce a clear answer to the question 'What character does Shakespeare mean his Brutus to be?'[17] In fact, the very first sentence of the soliloquy admits of several interpretations. Is it intended as the conclusion of preceding deliberations, indicating that at this early point the firm resolve to murder Caesar has already been established? Or is it more in the nature of a postulate that Brutus then seeks to justify with what follows?[18]

Almost all critics agree, however, that this laboured attempt to justify the preventive murder lacks conviction, that the arguments adduced by Brutus are founded on forgone conclusions and mere suppositions, that they are not based on Brutus's own experience of his friend Caesar or on what has been made known about him (11, 19–21) but rather on general abstract considerations.[19] Instead of providing from the past concrete proofs of Caesar's ambition, Brutus opts for platitudinous generalizations about the customary repercussions of ambition among those in high station. His reasoning is clearly not based on what is, but on what at some later date might be. The frequency of 'might', 'may', 'would' is an indication of the hypothetical mode of thought; Brutus weakens his own case with the admission 'to speak truth of Caesar, / I have not known when his affections sway'd / More than his reason' (19–21). While the frankness with which Brutus himself admits this patent contradiction inclines us in his favour, we balk at his renewed attempt to make the murder seem a necessity, justifiable to the general public (27 ff). The phrase 'Fashion it thus' arouses our suspicion, as it indicates a certain manipulation of the truth for the sake of justifying the deed in the eyes of the people. This is followed by mere hypotheses, and finally by a precarious analogy with the serpent's egg, which hardly seems applicable to this particular case and which magnifies the putative difference between the present and the future Caesar out of all proportion. We have the impression that the last word has not yet been said, and that Brutus must once more work up to the resolve announced at the beginning of the speech. The style and structure of the soliloquy reveal his inner uncertainty and his painful struggle to endorse a clear decision which will admit of no further doubt. As well as the pseudo-logic of the compound sentence structure with its 'buts' and 'ifs' we may discern a stylistic feature which is even more noticeable in the later speech in the forum, namely a kind of laconic compression: 'so Caesar may; / Then, lest he may, prevent . . .' (27–8). As grammar and syntax suggest, Brutus is driving himself towards the ultimate conclusion: 'It must be by his death' (10).

The fundamental attitudes which this soliloquy leads us to regard as typical of Brutus also arouse certain misgivings.[20] Brutus, the idealist, the responsible patriot, rates 'the general good' (12) higher than friendship, and is therefore willing to make the personal sacrifice of murdering his friend in order, as he thinks, to save Rome. But is not murder always murder? And is it possible to carry out a bloody deed as 'sacrificers, but not butchers' (166), as Brutus later demands? And is the appeal to higher values, characteristic of Brutus here and at other times, not self-deluding, unless it is combined with sober appraisal of reality? We too, as audience or readers, are confronted with these questions, and our attention is drawn to the major issues of the play; we are faced with the dilemma of whether the politically active man can remain without guilt and whether there are two sets of moral standards.

The impression of Brutus created by his first soliloquy is indeed an inconsistent one, but this is in all probability exactly what Shakespeare intended. Not only is Brutus in a dilemma, he is one of those characters, to appear fairly frequently in Shakespeare's plays from this point on, who provoke a mixed response.[21] He wavers uneasily between two viewpoints, and his uneasiness is transmitted to us. This becomes clearer still in the two subsequent passages of monologue. Brutus reads the letter brought in by Lucius without for a moment questioning its authenticity; his gullibility prompts us to question his intelligence. Shakespeare departs here significantly from his source: Plutarch mentions authentic letters of appeal from friends and citizens, whereas in the play Cassius had previously disclosed his design to lay anonymous letters on the window ledge by night, commenting to himself: 'For who so firm that cannot be seduc'd' (I.ii.309). Just as had been planned the three imperatives 'Speak, strike, redress' confirm Brutus in his lofty patriotic sentiments. Invoking his forefathers, he interprets the challenge to 'redress' as an obligation towards Rome which he promises to fulfil – a further step towards the 'ritualization' of Caesar's murder. This too is a tragic error on Brutus's part; the opening scene of the play had demonstrated that the people are by no means suffering under the yoke of oppression.

The next soliloquy (61 ff) shows us again that the decision to carry out the murder is reached only after great torment. It is no longer a matter of abstract considerations, with a touch of self-righteousness, as in the first soliloquy, but a deep inner conflict, 'a phantasma or a hideous dream', presented to us in the extended figure of the insurrection in the state of man. A different speech rhythm emerges in these disturbing lines.[22] We see before us a suffering human being whose conscience is deeply perturbed by the murder to which he has just consented. Something within him asserts itself against this resolve, and will not be denied. Our sympathy, lessened perhaps during the first soliloquy, is aroused anew,[23] and the words that he spoke to Cassius during the second scene, 'poor Brutus with himself at war' (I.ii.45), may well spring to mind at this moment. Again, these personal lines, which enable us to look into Brutus's heart and see his suffering, quickly give way to general statements. The opening lines of the soliloquy remind us of that momentous, tentative conversation between Brutus and Cassius, and establish a dramatic link between past and present. They focus our awareness on a psychological problem which was hinted at in the earlier scene. At the end of the conversation, which was designed to win him over to the conspiracy, Brutus had not committed himself; he had asked for time to consider his decision (I.ii.163 ff). Now we hear how deeply affected he has been by the proposition put to him by Cassius, how it has deprived him of sleep. The actual answer to the overtures made by Cassius in that dialogue (which scarcely was one, since Brutus was hardly a party to it), is only given now, in this third soliloquy.

The soliloquy is remarkable for yet another reason. A structural principle of the late tragedies following *Julius Caesar* becomes evident: it is not the criminal act, the central event of the plot, that provides the real focus of the play, but what takes place within the tragic hero before and after this act. Brutus's soliloquies demonstrate that 'drama' in Shakespeare means inner drama as well as outer events, particularly in the later plays.[24]

Brutus's last soliloquy, his invocation of Conspiracy, is interesting for several reasons too. For the first time he invokes an abstract term, which he personifies in order to confront it. In the morality play, such personifications of virtues and vices and other abstractions had frequently appeared on stage; Shakespeare continues the tradition, although his personifications more often appear as figures of speech rather than as actual characters. For his contemporaries, familiar with allegorical patterns of thought, such personifications represented a wide range of ethical and intellectual concepts which governed human existence.[25] Such apostrophes occur frequently at crucial points in the play when the abstract idea is of immediate relevance to the action. In this case Brutus has resolved to join the conspiracy, indeed to be its leader. He knows that conspiracy will mean murder. His invocation of Conspiracy is ambivalent and once more reveals his inner dilemma. Self-indictment and distaste for the enforced deceit are combined with the request to Conspiracy to assist them in their strategy. Brutus has to rely on the sheltering darkness of the night to give protection to the conspirators. Noble and upright as he is, he is forced into secrecy and dishonesty, has to follow a path from which his inner self recoils. He has to join the company of men whose goal, the liberating of Rome, he applauds, while abhorring their tactics. These conflicting thoughts about Conspiracy cast a shadow over the ensuing discussion. Although Brutus shows himself to be not only approachable but even cooperative and encouraging, we know of his ambivalent attitude towards the undertaking, and its dubiousness is revealed to the audience more and more clearly from this time on. The soliloquy has drawn an invisible dividing line between Brutus and the other conspirators; without it the audience's understanding of the meeting, which is continued until dawn, would have been quite different.

This soliloquy is also an example of Shakespeare's skill in providing a transition between the concrete and the abstract levels, linking the apostrophe to Conspiracy with the nocturnal hour and other details of the situation, such as the arrival of the masked conspirators. When Lucius returns he says of those waiting at the door: 'their hats are pluck'd about their ears, / And half their faces buried in their cloaks' (73–4). These comments are transferred directly to the evocation of Conspiracy, and the notion of the protective night in which evil can walk unseen is borrowed from the concrete situation. In establishing these links Brutus has already involved himself, has stigmatized himself as a participant in this dark alliance and indicted himself.

Although the sequence of soliloquies does not make up even a quarter of the scene, its effect on us and its importance for the understanding of the tragedy as a whole are immense. Brutus has moved into the centre of the action; we have been given some indication of his inner conflict and of the errors he is prone to make, and we are prepared to follow everything that he says, does or leaves undone with increased interest. Moreover, his speeches have given us cause to reflect on the fundamental political and moral issues raised in the play.

Hamlet

HAMLET'S SOLILOQUIES: INTRODUCTORY SURVEY

The seven soliloquies spoken by Hamlet[26] show Shakespeare at the peak of his powers with regard to the art of the soliloquy. Throughout the first four acts they provide a link between the inner and the outer action, and their occurrence at irregular intervals also contributes to the dramatic rhythm of the play, effecting a caesura, a moment for reflection, at important points. Without them an important dimension in the play would be missing; Hamlet's character would be even less comprehensible, and audience and reader would be less able to experience the tension of the play and to gain insight into its problems. Because of the special quality of the soliloquies and their difference from one another, it seems appropriate to preface the detailed examination of two speeches with a more general survey.

The first question is: why are soliloquies particularly necessary in *Hamlet*? Why does the audience look forward to these moments in which the protagonist can express his thoughts openly and honestly, and why are there far more motives for this intimacy and this form of self-expression in *Hamlet* than in other plays?

Not only is Hamlet one of the lonely heroes presented to us in Shakespeare's tragedies; he becomes progressively more isolated from and misunderstood by those around him. That is not only because he is different from the outset, but also because he has put on a mask (the 'antic disposition') and is playing a part. Other characters in the play are also dissembling, notably Claudius and Gertrude, and thus the necessity of Hamlet's disguise becomes all the more evident. Because he cannot speak freely to anyone, except Horatio, he has to speak cryptically. While he can see through others most acutely, he must on no account let others see through him, and yet there are truths which he is anxious to convey. This results in the indirect and roundabout remarks which startle and baffle his opponents.[27] We sense that beneath the surface of these veiled exchanges, which only occasionally lead to mutual understanding or to direct confrontation (as in the conversation between Hamlet and his mother, III.iv), there are hidden emotions which the other characters do not even guess at. As soon as he is left alone Hamlet feels the urge to break out of this unnatural situation and to speak his mind. We share both the relief that he experiences in solitude and the need that he feels to watch his tongue in company. The third soliloquy begins 'Now I am alone' (II.ii.543) – thus Hamlet reacts to the strain of being watched and drawn into superficial talk. The first soliloquy, on the other hand, ended with the words 'But break, my heart, for I must hold my tongue' (I.ii.159). It is the audience's prerogative to know Hamlet as he really is that gives these soliloquies their special impact. A feeling of intimacy develops which is denied to all Hamlet's fellow-players except Horatio. This does not mean that the soliloquies provide a key to all the secrets of Hamlet's character. The clarifying function of the soliloquy which was central at an earlier phase in the development of the drama is restricted in *Hamlet* to a few passages. Each soliloquy gives rise to new questions and some soliloquies contain contradictions of earlier utterances. Hamlet's character remains enigmatic[28] in spite of the many revealing statements we hear from him.

Nevertheless there are things to be learnt from the soliloquies that cannot be learnt from other parts of the text. Without the soliloquies we would scarcely know anything of Hamlet's self-accusations, of the way he is torn by conflicting moods, of his horror at his mother's incestuous marriage (at the very beginning of the play) and of his shock at the revelations of the ghost, of his promise to avenge his father's death, of his hatred for Claudius. We would only suspect these things, and we would have no clear idea of the major issue of the play, of Hamlet's delaying, if we did not have the soliloquies.[29]

The soliloquies make us aware of inner conflicts which at times develop into action, but it also becomes evident that Hamlet is powerless to resolve them. It is true that he submits himself in the soliloquies to merciless self-interrogation, usually caused by the sight of something or someone of sufficient contrast with himself to make him realize what he himself can never be (as for instance in the third soliloquy, II.ii.543 ff, or in the last one, IV.iv.32 ff). He indulges in self-accusations, and asks 'What am I?', but his self-analysis, in which modern readers may well recognize themselves, is inconclusive, for he does not understand himself. The uncertainties which assail him when he contemplates those close to him, and the world at large, apply equally to himself; he knows that his nature encompasses evil as well as good.

In several of the soliloquies (the first three and the last) this self-confrontation becomes a self-dramatization, inviting the actor to explore the theatrical potential,[30] for the text contains indications both of gestures and movements and of changes in tempo. Often, however, self-dramatization means overstatement. At times Hamlet seems to work himself up to extremes of mood, to cascades of words. His self-assessments at such moments are applicable to these particular occasions only and less objectively reliable than those given in the soliloquies of many other plays.[31]

A reading of the seven soliloquies in sequence will impress upon us their variety of mood, content and movement. This is not only a matter of context, but also of

Hamlet's contradictory state of mind, which can change completely from one soliloquy to the next. There is a particularly striking contrast between the third soliloquy (II.ii.543ff) and the fourth ('To be or not to be', see p. 132). Again the prevailing moods of the fifth and sixth soliloquies are quite different from the despairing cries of the first three, which all begin, significantly, with 'O . . .'.

The variations in mood are matched by variations in style. Hamlet's other speeches also display a wide range of styles, but in the soliloquies these differences are even more marked, and they are compressed into a shorter space. Above all we see how the turmoil, the violent emotions that erupt in Hamlet when he is alone, may lead to a dislocation of syntax as well as to a disruption of coherent thought. In dialogue Hamlet usually seems to adjust consciously to the other speaker, but in the soliloquies he abandons himself to the thoughts and ideas crowding in on him and sometimes overwhelming him, so that on several occasions he loses control of the flow of language. Sometimes he breaks off in mid-stream,[32] sometimes he returns to previously uttered oaths or phrases, as if the ideas would not let him go (as, for instance, in the first soliloquy). This gives a sense of spontaneous passionate speech being used to express reactions of the moment, sometimes before logical patterns of language have been imposed on them.

In the soliloquies it becomes apparent that Hamlet is fighting not only against the world around him but also against the overpowering strength of his own emotions, against the antagonism in his own heart. On the other hand, he is able to make the transition from the throes of despair to clear planning and decision-taking as, for instance, in the third soliloquy when at the end he hits on the idea of having the play performed before the king (II.ii.584 ff). Here, in fact, the transition from cries of outrage to the devising of new plans is achieved with the greatest economy:

> Fie upon't! Foh!
> About, my brains. Hum – I have heard . . .
>
> (II.ii.583–4)

The diction of what follows is very different from that of the preceding fragments of excited exclamation. In fact, it is the case in most of the soliloquies that we find measured and balanced lines reflecting Hamlet's moments of insight and sagacity beside clusters of questions or exclamations. It is one of his characteristics that he invariably sees beyond his own immediate concerns; his thoughts tend towards the universal in the individual. It is not by chance that many of his terse maxims are derived from proverbs familiar to the Elizabethans, or have in turn become household sayings (whereby a modern audience may not always be able to distinguish between the two). Such abrupt transitions to reflections on the world and mankind in general[33] occur in the dialogue too, particularly in the fifth Act where Hamlet has no more soliloquies, and yet speaks at times in a tone and style typical of them.

The variety of mood is accompanied by variations in tempo and intonation. The text indicates the rhythm, but there may still be several ways of speaking the lines. This is easily demonstrated if one compares the rendering of the soliloquies in different recordings, or if one reads them aloud to oneself.

Although Hamlet's soliloquies give expression to his inner conflict they also reflect the world and the people around him. Hamlet's father, his mother, Claudius, make their presence felt, and they come alive in the imagination partly by means of the comparisons with mythological figures (as for instance in the first soliloquy). Thus the term 'introspective' which is often used to describe the essence of the soliloquies is not entirely adequate. What Hamlet has just seen or experienced is shaped in the soliloquies into recollections, admonishments or mental confrontations with counterfigures against whom he tries to match himself. He has taken note of situations, certain gestures, even a particular facial expression, and his retentive memory holds on to them or re-creates them. In this way the hurt, loathing and despair inherent in these memories are reiterated. Yet what has imprinted itself most indelibly on his memory is the appearance of his father's ghost and the commandments issued by him. Three times in Hamlet's second soliloquy, which follows immediately upon the scene with the ghost, the keyword 'remember' occurs, ensuring that the audience too will keep in mind the ghost's last request, 'remember me' (I.v.91).

The occurrence of concrete sense perceptions in the soliloquies also acts as a link with the past, enabling us to re-live past events from Hamlet's point of view. At the same time we are alerted to the behaviour of the other actors in the ensuing scenes, even to their facial expressions, more than we would have been without this preparation. We are also better able to understand the meaning of Hamlet's cryptic statements with their allusions, veiled threats and implications.

In some places the audience are told explicitly what to look out for in a later scene, and it is clear that one function of the soliloquy really is to prepare us for things to come. Thus at the end of the third soliloquy Hamlet tells us what he is going to do when the play is performed before the king:

> I'll observe his looks;
> I'll tent him to the quick. If a do blench,
> I know my course.
>
> (II.ii.592 ff)

In the fifth soliloquy Hamlet reminds himself not to go too far in the impending conversation with his mother:

> Let me be cruel, not unnatural.
> I will speak daggers to her, but use none.
>
> (III.ii.386–7)

Not only will the audience recall these lines when the disturbing scene between mother and son takes place; they will also wonder whether Hamlet is going to keep within the bounds that he has set himself. In Shakespeare's soliloquies there have always been indications of later plot developments, but in *Hamlet* these indications constitute an imaginary anticipation of the things to come. Close examination of the first and fourth soliloquies will show how by gradual stages feeling and thinking, seeing and reflecting are interwoven with one another. This is true of most of the other soliloquies too; by the end of the speech Hamlet will have moved away from his starting-point. After the initial outburst of emotions, distinctive of the opening of the first three soliloquies, he wins his way through to a phase of questioning, comparing and reflecting. Usually the soliloquies occur at a moment when Hamlet has just been challenged to scrutinize himself and to react appropriately to a given situation. 'That would be scann'd . . .' (III.iii.75) is the opening of his reflections at the sight of Claudius sunk in prayer; to kill him at this moment, sending him to heaven rather than to hell, makes no sense to him. In the last soliloquy, spoken after the army led by Fortinbras has marched past, it is even more apparent that a visual impression has provoked Hamlet into contrasting the activity of others with his own inactivity. He questions the nature of man ('What is a man . . .'), twice contemplates himself (43 ff, 56 ff), and resolves to take vengeance ('O, from this time forth / My thoughts be bloody or be nothing worth' [65]). During the soliloquy there has been some inner change and at the end of it a different Hamlet stands before us, determined now to shed his enemy's blood.

It has been pointed out that the Hamlet of the late soliloquies (III.iii.73; IV.iv.32) is no longer the same as the earlier one. The wild despair which led to a dislocation of syntax in the first three soliloquies has given way to a calmer and more controlled mode of speech and thought.

Whether this should be taken to mean that in the latter stages of the play Shakespeare wanted to show us an older and more mature Hamlet, or whether we are simply seeing Hamlet in a different frame of mind – a change that we note in the transition from the third to the fourth soliloquy – must remain an open question. Nor do we feel the same degree of sympathy towards him at all times. His bloodthirsty oaths and affirmations in the fifth and sixth soliloquies, reflecting the tradition of the Elizabethan tragedy of revenge, may alienate many of us today, whereas the first four soliloquies have created an atmosphere of intimacy and trust.[34] Yet even the temporary lapse in confidence is in keeping with the fundamental purpose of the tragedy, which does not present us with any clear answers, but rather arouses in us those same doubts and uncertainties which assail the hero from the outset.

HAMLET'S REJECTION OF THE WORLD

I.ii.129–59

Flourish. Exeunt all but Hamlet.

Hamlet. O that this too too sullied flesh would melt,
    Thaw and resolve itself into a dew,   130
    Or that the Everlasting had not fix'd
    His canon 'gainst self-slaughter. O God! God!
    How weary, stale, flat, and unprofitable
    Seem to me all the uses of this world!
    Fie on't, ah fie, 'tis an unweeded garden   135
    That grows to seed; things rank and gross in nature
    Possess it merely. That it should come to this!
    But two months dead—nay, not so much, not two—
    So excellent a king, that was to this
    Hyperion to a satyr, so loving to my mother   140
    That he might not beteem the winds of heaven
    Visit her face too roughly. Heaven and earth,
    Must I remember? Why, she would hang on him
    As if increase of appetite had grown

By what it fed on; and yet within a month—   145
Let me not think on't—Frailty, thy name is woman—
A little month, or ere those shoes were old
With which she follow'd my poor father's body,
Like Niobe, all tears—why, she—
O God, a beast that wants discourse of reason   150
Would have mourn'd longer—married with my uncle,
My father's brother—but no more like my father
Than I to Hercules. Within a month,
Ere yet the salt of most unrighteous tears
Had left the flushing in her galled eyes,
She married—O most wicked speed! To post   155
With such dexterity to incestuous sheets!
It is not, nor it cannot come to good.
But break, my heart, for I must hold my tongue.

Hamlet's first soliloquy occurs in the middle of the scene in
which he makes his first appearance. He speaks only a few
lines before being left alone on the stage, but during the
ceremonial scene at court we already sense that what is
taking place within him differs starkly from what is going
on around him. To begin with he remains entirely in the
background, a figure of secondary importance, while in
the foreground King Claudius deals with affairs of state in
smooth and bland speeches, finally turning to his nephew
to admonish him with hollow, solicitous words. We are
able to recognize the duplicity in these lines; beneath the
initial friendliness lies a muted threat (95 ff). While
Claudius is speaking, our attention is drawn several times
to Hamlet's averted, mourning figure, which is also
rendered visually conspicuous by his black garb. The first
utterance with which he breaks his silence is not only an
aside (which in itself emphasizes his aloofness), it is also
cryptic and ambiguous, as is so much of what he has to say:
'A little more than kin, and less than kind' (I.ii.65). From
this laconic comment we gather at once that Hamlet sees

through the words addressed to him. This impression is confirmed by the longer speech that we hear from him shortly afterwards. In this Hamlet takes up the queen's word 'seems'. We are told that he has something in him which goes beyond the seeming of external mourning; but his words apply more widely to the opposition between appearance and reality[35] presented before us on the stage. This contrast will be one of the recurring themes of the play. Thus we are prepared in several ways for the soliloquy that is to follow: by the dramatic action which draws attention to Hamlet's aloofness; by the contrast between the outer display of court ceremony and the reality which we sense but cannot yet grasp; and finally by the self-exposure of Hamlet's own words.

The soliloquy provides no direct answer to the questions which have been shaping themselves during the scene, and such answer as there is emerges only at the end. During the first nine lines we do not even know what experience it is that has plunged Hamlet into the depths of despair. Moreover we were expecting him to speak of the loss of his inheritance and the usurpation of the throne by his uncle, a matter which will not have escaped the notice of an Elizabethan audience and which is alluded to later on. At this point nothing is said about it. Only at the end of the soliloquy do we hear the words which explain Hamlet's horrified reactions to his mother's overhasty marriage: 'incestuous sheets' (157). According to a view commonly held at the time, marriage to the brother of the deceased husband was incest.[36]

What we hear when Hamlet first begins to speak alone is a maelstrom of the most diverse perceptions, reflections and emotions, in which love and reverence for his father mingle with grief, anger and despair about his mother. The style and structure of this soliloquy contrasts sharply with the ordered and balanced utterances of the king. Unfinished sentences, exclamations, interruptions, questions, repetitions and abrupt transitions are the syntactic signs of this outburst of passion, but in spite of the emotional turmoil we are given an extraordinary amount of detailed information, not only about Hamlet's state of mind but also about the world around him, which is mirrored with great precision. Very little is stated in abstract terms in this soliloquy; for the most part, both thought and feeling are given concrete form; audience and reader are presented with an abundance of sense impressions. Since much of this draws on matters previously unknown to us, our eyes are opened to a whole network of interrelationships. In this way the soliloquy contributes to the exposition of the plot.

The soliloquy begins with Hamlet's death wish, which is not to be taken as a wish to escape into the beyond, but as a desire for the dissolution of the self, visualized in the image of the melting flesh, and displays Hamlet's tendency to anchor his thoughts in the body.[37] The very next line discountenances the fulfilment of this wish, since God's commandment forbids suicide. It is revealing that Hamlet's series of seven soliloquies opens with the thought of death and suicide. Both themes recur in various forms in the tragedy (not only in the fourth soliloquy) and they belong to the play's leitmotifs.

The following lines, in which Hamlet gives us his impressions of the world, also tell us something about his manner of perceiving and judging. In four pejorative adjectives 'weary, stale, flat, and unprofitable' (133) he makes known his disgust, and then he immediately turns his subjective perceptions into a general assessment of the world with the notable image of the 'Unweeded garden / That grows to seed' (135–6). Thus the soliloquy opens not only with Hamlet's death-wish but also with his affirmation that he is turning his back on the world, resigning all hope. At this stage he has not even learnt of the event that will shake him most profoundly, the murder of his father. We may wonder whether such a man will find strength to act when the call to action comes.

Only from line 137 onwards does Hamlet reveal to us the

concrete details of what has prompted his outburst of despair. In the way in which feelings, thoughts and perceptions are blended and presented in the dislocated syntax, Shakespeare's art in handling the soliloquy reaches a new, higher level.[38] In the passages previously discussed we had some interruptions, exclamations and questions, but never such a mixture of disparate elements rising forcefully and almost simultaneously to the surface. Long before it was discovered by modern psychology, Shakespeare knew that in an over-sensitive person close to despair the impressions and feelings that have not been worked through and assimilated erupt into consciousness, resulting not in cohesive thought or in the ability to discriminate between more and less important matters, but in a kaleidoscopic mingling of overpowering and volatile emotions. Hamlet is overwhelmed by memories of his parents' love for one another (140 ff), of his mother's mourning as she followed his father's body 'like Niobe, all tears' (149); he tries to control them but cannot prevent them from imprinting themselves with painful clarity – another manifestation of the conflict within him.

As we have already seen, Shakespeare found diverse means of dramatizing his soliloquies. Here is another. The accompaniment of these intrusive memories by the re-creation of typical gestures, facial expressions and setting, enables the audience to comprehend exactly what it is that is being recalled. Already in this first soliloquy we have evidence of Hamlet's extraordinarily powerful memory. The interpolated exclamation 'Must I remember' (143) gives some indication of the important part played by his memory, his 'inner eye', his inability to forget.

The first cry of horror introducing the dramatic argument of the soliloquy, 'That it should come to this!' (137), is a fitting preparation for what follows; over and over again Hamlet compares what he sees with what he once saw. For him the debasement of the mother he has loved is epitomized in the brief span of time which elapsed between his father's death and her remarriage. He refers to it four times. The first time he corrects himself about the exact length of time: 'But two months dead – nay, not so much, not two' (138). The sense of immediacy is accompanied by a strong sense of tangible reality, illustrated by references to 'ere those shoes were old / with which she followed my poor father's body' (147) and to the 'salt of most unrighteous tears' (154) that still lingered in her eyes; these become the unforgettable emblems of the brevity of her mourning. When the thought of this short month agitates him for the fourth time, 'Within a month . . .' (153), and he breaks off in mid-sentence and cries out in the utmost disgust: 'O most wicked speed! To post / With such dexterity to incestuous sheets!' (156–7), we realize what lies behind his reaction to the brevity of mourning. We understand more clearly why it is that this soliloquy throbs with such violent emotion, leading, after the initial memories of his mother, to the general condemnation of all women (just as judgement was passed on the whole world earlier on): 'Let me not think on't – Frailty, thy name is woman –' (146). As often happens in Shakespeare, earlier words are elucidated by later ones. This is true even within the space of a single soliloquy.

In this speech Hamlet's father, Claudius and Gertrude are referred to one after another, and each time we can learn much from the hero's vision of them. 'So excellent a king, that was to this / Hyperion to a satyr' (139–40): this, together with the lines that follow, not only tells us how Hamlet revered his father but also introduces the sequence of contrasts between King Hamlet and Claudius that is sustained right through the play, culminating in the scene in Gertrude's bedroom (III.iv). A second contrast occurs in this soliloquy: 'My father's brother – but no more like my father / Than I to Hercules' (152–3).[39] The audience take note, readjusting the impressions created by what has been seen and heard in previous scenes, and the later scenes are observed with an altered perspective even though the audience may have reservations about Hamlet's judgement at some points.

The last line but one, 'It is not, nor it cannot come to good' (158), is a summing up, expressing an ominous presentiment. Although this conclusion is in keeping with the conventions of the soliloquy, it strikes us with its remarkable simplicity and a succinctness rarely achieved before. The last line marks the end of Hamlet's freedom to speak openly, since the encounter with those who are already seen approaching will once more demand a withdrawal into reticence. The tone of the first line of the soliloquy is echoed in 'But break my heart' (one of Hamlet's many self-addressed utterances), and the oppression of spirit which has pervaded the whole speech will stay with him throughout the following dialogue.

HAMLET'S 'TO BE, OR NOT TO BE'
III.i.56–90

Enter HAMLET.

Ham. To be, or not to be, that is the question:
    Whether 'tis nobler in the mind to suffer
    The slings and arrows of outrageous fortune,
    Or to take arms against a sea of troubles
    And by opposing end them. To die—to sleep,   60
    No more; and by a sleep to say we end
    The heart-ache and the thousand natural shocks
    That flesh is heir to: 'tis a consummation
    Devoutly to be wish'd. To die, to sleep;
    To sleep, perchance to dream—ay, there's the rub: 65
    For in that sleep of death what dreams may come,
    When we have shuffled off this mortal coil,
    Must give us pause—there's the respect
    That makes calamity of so long life.

For who would bear the whips and scorns of time,   70
Th'oppressor's wrong, the proud man's contumely,
The pangs of dispriz'd love, the law's delay,
The insolence of office, and the spurns
That patient merit of th'unworthy takes,
When he himself might his quietus make   75
With a bare bodkin? Who would fardels bear,
To grunt and sweat under a weary life,
But that the dread of something after death,
The undiscover'd country, from whose bourn
No traveller returns, puzzles the will,   80
And makes us rather bear those ills we have
Than fly to others that we know not of?
Thus conscience does make cowards of us all,
And thus the native hue of resolution
Is sicklied o'er with the pale cast of thought,   85
And enterprises of great pitch and moment
With this regard their currents turn awry
And lose the name of action. Soft you now,
The fair Ophelia! Nymph, in thy orisons
Be all my sins remember'd.

This is the most famous of Shakespeare's soliloquies,
indeed of all soliloquies, and it is also the one for which the
greatest number of interpretations have been offered.[40] In
style and structure it is less typical of Shakespeare than
those examined hitherto. The dovetailing with the dramatic action is less apparent; thus what has seemed to be
distinctively characteristic of Shakespeare's soliloquies is
lacking here. Though other soliloquies have centred on
reflection, they have involved other elements as well: sense
perceptions, self-observation or observation of the environ-
ment, anticipation of future events, purposeful planning,
concrete recollections and reactions to the immediate past.
Most soliloquies are designed to reveal the intentions of the
speaker, to unveil what is hidden, but here the audience

is given no answer to all the play's unsolved problems; rather, new questions arise. Hamlet's doubts spread to the audience.

Confronted with a text apparently lacking in logical and syntactic cohesion, most of the numerous (several hundred!) interpretations of this soliloquy have tried to supply the missing links, to clarify the sense, to give precision to what has merely been hinted at. Such endeavours, which reveal both the strengths and the weaknesses of philological explication, neglect Shakespeare's probable intentions at this point, for the particular effect of this soliloquy is founded on the very fact that the cohesion is not explicit. In this instance, as so often in Shakespeare, the implicit is more effective than the explicit.

Moreover, the apparent lack of connections between the soliloquy and what precedes and follows it is what makes it particularly effective in a good production. Everything is different from before and, nevertheless, or perhaps precisely for this reason, we are deeply moved.

Instead of textual analysis proceeding line by line, trying to answer the question, 'What does Hamlet actually mean here?', a different approach will be used in an attempt to determine what, above all, imprints itself on our minds when we hear this soliloquy, what is conveyed to our imagination and emotions by the movement of the verse, the diction and the imagery; and what is meant when a soliloquy begins and ends so abruptly, just as we were expecting something quite different to happen.[41]

We begin with the last of these and try to re-create the expectations of the audience when Hamlet returns to the stage. Only a few minutes have elapsed since we heard the soliloquy at the end of the second act, in which he was reacting to the First Player's 'Hecuba speech', which had displayed attitudes and deeds so contrary to his own that he felt them to be a direct challenge. At the end of the soliloquy he had conceived the plan of ascertaining the guilt of the king by means of a play to be performed by the actors (II.ii.584–601). In the next scene we first hear a conversation between Claudius and his entourage, concerned with Hamlet and his enigmatic behaviour; our attention is still focused on him. Shortly before he enters, the king and Polonius hide in the background, continuing their attempt to spy on him. Whether or not they actually overhear the soliloquy we do not know, but something of the tense expectation with which the eavesdroppers await Hamlet's reappearance is communicated to the audience. What will Hamlet reveal? We expect a continuation of the thoughts expressed in the last soliloquy, some further development of his plans, but there is no more mention of that. Neither Claudius, nor the plans for the play, nor Gertrude is mentioned, nor indeed is there any reference to himself. A different Hamlet seems to stand before us. After the turmoil of the last soliloquy, Hamlet now seems to be governed by a great calm, to be distancing himself in contemplation both from himself and from what is happening around him, although we sense that deep within the torment still persists. Absorbed in thought he seems to be isolated from everything around him. The two eavesdroppers in their hiding place contrast ironically with his solitude, increasing even more the sympathy with which the audience listen to his words. His thoughts are not directed towards the here and now but towards the ultimate questions of man's existence. The audience, too, detach their thoughts for a while from the action of the drama, and pause to reflect. Thus in the middle of the play there is a caesura. Hamlet feels very close to death, but this has less to do with a threat from outside than with his existence as a human being. Thus the soliloquy contributes to the fundamental impression of delay and postponement determined by Hamlet's conduct.

Part of the soliloquy's effectiveness lies in its contrast with what precedes it: Shakespeare combines preparation with surprise. The first two acts prepare us for Hamlet's changes of character and his contradictory moods. Several times during his speeches passionate and specific concern has given way to philosophical contemplation.

The soliloquy is an important example of Hamlet's ability to think beyond the present, while on the other hand his own immediate concern is manifested only in a very indirect way, for he does not refer to himself at all. The 'first person' in this speech is plural and not singular; Hamlet is not actually talking to himself. Instead of 'I', 'my', 'me' we find 'we', 'our', 'us'. In contrast to his previous manner of speech, thoughts take shape slowly. In no other soliloquy do the audience have such a clear sense of being present at the conception of thoughts and ideas. The process of seeking, reflecting and associating, which is interrupted before it progresses to intense concentration and focus, is what strikes the listener on first hearing this soliloquy. Both rhythm and sound contribute to the effect. The words of the soliloquy, however, show us only the crest of the wave; what lies between one crest and the next is often omitted, and has to be supplied by the attentive audience. Dr Johnson was one of the first to recognize that the train of thought is linked deep beneath the surface when he spoke of it as being 'connected rather in the speaker's mind, than on his tongue'.[42]

Scarcely any other soliloquy of Shakespeare's is open to so many different manners of delivery; the actor can direct the thoughts of the audience this way or that, depending on the emphasis and tempo that he chooses.[43]

The query with which Hamlet begins this soliloquy, 'To be, or not to be', has become so familiar that we have to ask ourselves with renewed awareness what its effect at this particular point in the play may have been. According to an established though not demonstrably early tradition, Hamlet enters the stage deeply absorbed in reading a book, putting his question as a comment on what he has just been reading. We shall be reminded several times during the play of this twofold view of Hamlet as the Wittenberg student, at home in the world of learning, pondering on what he has been reading, and yet called upon to take prompt action.

Even more important is that the weighing and balancing of one alternative against another which is expressed in this famous opening line is continued throughout the soliloquy, without any conclusion ever being drawn. Hamlet uses the interrogative form with striking frequency.[44] It is particularly characteristic of him, expressing both the doubts and uncertainties that assail him with regard to the past and his inability to decide on a future course of action. The contemplation of two equally unacceptable alternatives is expressed here in the form of a keenly felt and yet generalized meditation, valid for all mankind. The listener senses that a fundamental problem affecting his own existence is being stated, he feels himself drawn into Hamlet's consideration of the ultimate questions of mankind. The preoccupation of modern man – his dilemmas, vain quests and searchings – are confirmed. The great art and particular effect of this soliloquy lie in the way in which the tone of personal pain and loss as well as the expressiveness and imaginative powers so typical of Hamlet are retained, and yet at the same time the personal is elevated to the level of the universal.

In the soliloquy various grammatical structures can be discerned which help to convey this twofold impression. The uncertainty is expressed in a series of infinitive forms.[45] 'To be, or not to be' is followed by 'to suffer', 'to take arms', 'to say', 'to die', 'to sleep', 'to dream', 'to grunt and sweat'. The non-finite form enables the speaker to hold himself at a distance from the action. The frequent questions are countered by further questions and objections, but the liberating step to an answer which would resolve the dilemma is never taken. The possible alternatives which become visible for a moment are rejected, not viable for the mind that thinks beyond the moment and sees the consequences of action.

The inner drama of the soliloquy is reinforced by the fact that not all the utterances are well-balanced antithetical constructions; after nine lines the flow of thought is checked. It lingers before reaching out towards new insight, which in turn ends in a feeling of futility. We hear the full conviction of 't'is a consummation devoutly to be wished',[46] and the unusual use of 'consummation', derived from liturgical texts, and 'devoutly' add something of a religious tone. But then the tempo is checked by the four infinitives already listed: 'To die, to sleep; / To sleep, perchance to dream'. The thoughts advance, but progress is blocked, and the obstacle is indicated by the colloquial brusqueness of 'ay, there's the rub'. All this within the space of a mere three lines (63–5).

There is another caesura in the sense as well as in the verse when the next sentence ends with the accented 'pause', to be followed not by a weakly stressed syllable but by 'There's', also fully accented. The phrase 'Must give us pause' (68) is indicative of Hamlet's disposition, as of the whole play, but here the pause is on the threshold of eternity. There is another brief phrase, 'puzzles the will' (80), which, although it is again used with reference to mankind in general, is relevant to Hamlet's particular problem, 'puzzles' having a much stronger meaning in Elizabethan English than it has now ('bewilders so as to make incapable of proceeding', see New Arden).

The other factor which gives this soliloquy a tone of personal grief is the imagery which alerts us to Hamlet's own suffering and vulnerability, although the speech refers to the travail and frustrations of life in general. Both 'to suffer / The slings and arrows of outrageous fortune' (57–8) and 'to take arms against a sea of troubles' (59) combine images from the battle-field with abstract notions, suggesting, firstly, continuous threat and, secondly, the hopeless, doomed battle against an all-powerful enemy. The word 'nobler' arrests our attention because it makes plain the moral perspective from which Hamlet contemplates the alternatives, but at the same time we realize that none of these courses is really viable, that there is still no escape.[47] The first four lines already exemplify the dual effect of the soliloquy, appealing to the imagination as well as to the intellect, and challenging the audience to active participation.

The inescapability of suffering still prevails in the second part of the soliloquy. The verb 'to bear' replaces 'to suffer' (70, 76, 81), while 'the whips and scorns of time' (70) parallels 'the slings and arrows of outrageous fortune', expressing the inequity that man must daily endure. A little earlier come the two famous lines expressing the wretchedness of life on earth in all its physical immediacy: 'The heartache and the thousand natural shocks / That flesh is heir to' (62–3). A little later the process of dying is presented as physical liberation from earthly affliction ('when we have shuffled off this mortal coil')[48] in a manner which combines material and mental concepts; but primal bodily sensations are expressed most drastically in the final question, in the image of man being forced to bear the load of human existence like a beast of burden: 'Who would fardels bear, / To grunt and sweat under a weary life . . .' (76–7). The lower level of phrasing is in marked contrast with the elevated diction of 'quietus', a learned word used just before with reference to suicide. The preceding lines display yet another way of expressing the suffering imposed by the world; in six successive phrases, which categorize human behaviour and social standing, Hamlet enumerates the injustices and miseries continually inflicted on mankind (although he himself, in his privileged position as prince, would hardly have been affected). The whole passage is an example of abstraction giving way to the immediacy of detail.

The 'bare bodkin' concretizes the idea of suicide, and

the audience realizes that Hamlet has reached the crux of the soliloquy; but this last escape route also is rejected, and again it is uncertainty – this time of what will happen after death – that causes the rejection. For centuries people have debated as to whether Hamlet is considering killing himself at this point, or just citing a possibility offered to every man. Why should not both meanings be intended? In contemplating a way of escape which occurs sooner or later to all who seek to evade earthly suffering, he will have numbered himself among those to whom this possibility is open.

An abstract problem is presented in physical terms again in the last few lines (before Hamlet catches sight of Ophelia) and these lines have been discussed even more frequently than the earlier part of the soliloquy:

> Thus conscience does make cowards of us all,
> And thus the native hue of resolution
> Is sicklied o'er with the pale cast of thought,
> And enterprises of great pitch and moment
> With this regard their currents turn awry,
> And lose the name of action.
>
> (III.i.83–8)

The keywords 'resolution' and 'action' have led some commentators to suggest that in this soliloquy Hamlet has worked his way through to a final vision which should be understood as a decision to act, a solution to the earlier dilemma which can now be left behind; but this can hardly be proved. Hamlet never gives us the final piece of information which he would perhaps have given – the sight of Ophelia causes him to break off. We can be sure that at the end of the soliloquy Shakespeare wanted us still to be unsure about the conclusion that Hamlet himself would have drawn from his meditation.

These final lines offer an incomparable image for the dilemma of every man who is called to action and who yet consults his conscience and reflects. What Goethe was later to formulate in abstract terms in his *Maximen und Reflexionen* ('Man in action is always without conscience; none but the thinker has a conscience'), Shakespeare transposes into metaphor with his distinctively psycho-physical vision, highlighting the figurative opposition of sickness and health which is characteristic of Hamlet and also of the whole play.[49] We realize that although these lines also are formulated in general and neutral terms, almost as a maxim might be, yet they describe his own problem. The passage has rightly been regarded as a vital one for the understanding of the play.

The tender and affectionate words which Hamlet quietly speaks at the end of the soliloquy when he sees Ophelia, unheard by and yet addressed to her, create the transition to the scene which follows. The mood and style change significantly, but so also does the picture of Hamlet's character which the soliloquy has helped us to form. What follows presents us with the most abrupt and disturbing change in the whole play, and it is certainly no accident that this particular soliloquy has preceded it.

Macbeth

LADY MACBETH READS HER HUSBAND'S LETTER
I.v.1–30

Enter LADY MACBETH, *reading a letter.*

Lady M. "They met me in the day of success; and I
have learn'd by the perfect'st report, they have
more in them than mortal knowledge. When I
burn'd in desire to question them further, they
made themselves air, into which they vanish'd.   5
Whiles I stood rapt in the wonder of it, came
missives from the King, who all-hail'd me, 'Thane
of Cawdor'; by which title, before, these Weird
Sisters saluted me, and referr'd me to the coming

on of time, with 'Hail, King that shalt be!' This
have I thought good to deliver thee (my dearest   10
partner of greatness) that thou might'st not lose the
dues of rejoicing, by being ignorant of what
greatness is promis'd thee. Lay it to thy heart, and
farewell."
Glamis thou art, and Cawdor; and shalt be   15
What thou art promis'd.—Yet do I fear thy nature:
It is too full o' th' milk of human kindness,
To catch the nearest way. Thou wouldst be great;
Art not without ambition, but without
The illness should attend it: what thou wouldst highly,
That wouldst thou holily; wouldst not play false,   21
And yet wouldst wrongly win; thou'dst have, great
    Glamis,
That which cries, "Thus thou must do," if thou have
it;
And that which rather thou dost fear to do,
Than wishest should be undone. Hie thee hither,   25
That I may pour my spirits in thine ear,
And chastise with the valour of my tongue
All that impedes thee from the golden round,
Which fate and metaphysical aid doth seem
To have thee crown'd withal.

LADY MACBETH'S PACT WITH THE INFERNAL POWERS
I.v.38–54
                                    The raven
        himself is hoarse,
    That croaks the fatal entrance of Duncan
    Under my battlements. Come, you Spirits   40
    That tend on mortal thoughts, unsex me here,
    And fill me, from the crown to the toe, top-full
    Of direst cruelty! make thick my blood,
    Stop up th' access and passage to remorse;
    That no compunctious visitings of Nature   45

Shake my fell purpose, nor keep peace between
Th' effect and it! Come to my woman's breasts,
And take my milk for gall, you murth'ring ministers,
Wherever in your sightless substances
You wait on Nature's mischief! Come, thick Night,   50
And pall thee in the dunnest smoke of Hell,
That my keen knife see not the wound it makes,
Nor Heaven peep through the blanket of the dark,
To cry, "Hold, hold!"

The first soliloquy in the play is spoken not by Macbeth
but by his wife.[50] If we examine it, bearing in mind
Macbeth's great soliloquy in the last scene of the first act,
we see how important it is for the understanding of this
later scene, for which Shakespeare prepares us on several
different levels. In *Macbeth*, even more so than in the other
tragedies, what is said in one scene supplements and
connects with what is said in another, so that hardly any
passage can be examined in isolation without losing the
associations which are necessary for a full understanding.
Before each of the great soliloquies Shakespeare creates a
tissue of expectations, contradictory impressions and press-
ing questions in the mind of the reader or audience; but we
can give only a few indications of this cohesion since a full
demonstration would exceed the scope of this study.

When Lady Macbeth makes her first entry she is reading
her husband's letter aloud,[51] indirectly introducing herself
in soliloquy via the words of another. Both Lady Macbeth
and Macbeth are characterized by the letter, Macbeth
inasmuch as he keeps back the important fact that Banquo
was also present at the meeting with the witches and
received a prophecy which might well thwart his own
expectations. Macbeth records the witches' decisive
prophecy 'Hail, King that shalt be' without drawing any
conclusions and without betraying anything of the com-
pulsive fantasy which has already laid hold of his imagi-

nation. Only the phrase with which he addresses his wife immediately afterwards – 'my dearest partner of greatness' – anticipates the future. When a great actress plays the part of Lady Macbeth, the manner of reading the letter tells us a great deal about her character too.[52] When the letter quotes the witches' prophecy, something like a sudden enlightenment takes place within her, as she contemplates the undreamt-of prospect opening up before Macbeth and herself. She calculates at once what this must involve for the future and summarizes her realization succinctly and pragmatically in one-and-a-half lines, deliberately, however, avoiding the word 'king'. Thus the cryptic message of the letter has taken effect just as the writer in all probability intended; it is a veiled appeal to Lady Macbeth to utter the unspeakable and to plan the inconceivable.

Macbeth's letter calls to mind the third scene of the first act. As so often in his great plays, Shakespeare recalls earlier scenes when they are particularly important for subsequent events, or when we are being challenged to make comparisons. In this case, both apply; but how differently Macbeth and Lady Macbeth react to the witches' prophecy! Macbeth sinks into an almost trance-like state, manifested in several asides. These asides already have something of the quality of a soliloquy; they indicate the extent to which Macbeth's mind is appropriated and overwhelmed so that he is oblivious of others and begins to speak to himself. Murder is mentioned for the first time:

> My thought, whose murder yet is but fantastical
>
> (I.iii.139)

It is as if we were witnessing the conception of the thought of murdering Duncan. This thought, however, is accompanied by fear and uncertainty, by enormous trepidation and by the desire to evade ultimate responsibility. Lady Macbeth's soliloquy picks up all these threads, as does the first great soliloquy from Macbeth a little later.

After the reading of the letter Lady Macbeth addresses her absent partner, whose weaknesses she recognizes and enumerates as so many obstacles on the course which she herself is resolutely prepared to take, without scruple or delay (15–30). The dialogue within the monologue evokes Macbeth's presence. The lines are crucial to our understanding of the debate[53] that is to take place between them, and later on within Macbeth, above all in the soliloquy in I.vii. Again Shakespeare is achieving several different things simultaneously. The fateful partnership between Macbeth and Lady Macbeth, the specific interrelation of forces, is in evidence here for the first time, resulting in a dramatic confrontation in the second part of the scene. The soliloquy shows us how the temptation that approached Macbeth in the form of the witches is now laying hold of Lady Macbeth also, how in her the drive towards evil immediately assumes a definite shape, a clearly calculated plan of action. Above all, in a few lines, we are given an evaluation of Macbeth's weaknesses but also of his merits, which for the time being we are prepared to believe because it comes from someone who has an exact knowledge of him. The 'milk of human kindness' which Lady Macbeth refers to disparagingly, as being likely to forbid Macbeth 'to catch the nearest way', (certainly referring to the murder), is a trait that can incline us favourably towards him; this fundamental human quality prevents us from regarding him from the beginning as a cold villain incapable of compassion. Lady Macbeth, however, is also aware of her husband's propensity towards self-deception, towards deluding himself that there can be action without consequences, and that it is perfectly possible to come by unlawful winnings without having first played false. Her words also give the first hint that for Macbeth there is a deep chasm between the planning of an evil action and its execution. This same problem will come to the fore in his soliloquies and other comparable speeches. Lady Macbeth's voice, addressing her absent partner with a blend of cool analysis and relentless urgency, is overlaid half way through the soliloquy by the projection of a second voice, not human, which articulates Macbeth's guileful wish:

> thou'dst have, great Glamis,
> That which cries, 'Thus thou must do', if thou
> have it;
>
> $(22-3)^{54}$

Whereas in the first ten lines Lady Macbeth has spoken only of her husband, she now describes the influence that she herself intends to exert on him, significantly referring to 'poison' and 'chastisement'. The 'spirits' that she proposes to pour into his ear[55] are to inspire him with courage to do not good but evil. Her first soliloquy closes with the vision of Macbeth crowned with the 'golden round', and it leads us to surmise even at this early stage that Lady Macbeth's ambition exceeds that of her husband. Of course she knows, as the preceding lines show clearly, that will and ambition alone will not suffice. 'Fate and metaphysical aid' (29) (with the revealingly doubtful 'seem') point the way to the mysterious constellation out of which the tragedy will grow.

Her soliloquy is interrupted by the arrival of a messenger bringing news of the approach of the King and Macbeth, and only twenty-five lines later Macbeth himself enters. Expectations have been aroused and are sustained during the second soliloquy, which leads in a quite different direction; for only now does Lady Macbeth turn her attention resolutely towards herself. The fact that this happens so late is no accident, and it casts a significant light on the part that she plays in the tragedy.

There is an immense difference between her two soliloquies following so closely one upon the other. The first begins with the prose letter and then moves into blank verse for the dialogue with the absent partner; the flexible verse bears the stamp of a keen intellect and a pragmatic turn of mind, combining cool calculation with realistic analysis of the situation. The language is determined by reason, with a predominance of short balanced clauses, which contain hardly any imagery. In the second soliloquy there is a quite different world, full of demonic inner action, of symbolic images[56] and suggestive words and phrases to stimulate the imagination. It begins and ends with the evocation of atmosphere, conjuring up the fatal sombreness and terror of the night with animal cries and shrieks of fear.

What we experience in this second soliloquy is a deliberate act of dedication to evil, but evil can only take full possession of Lady Macbeth after her human nature, her femininity, has been driven out of her. This is the common purpose of the three challenges all beginning with 'Come'; they enable us to see that the inner transformation which Lady Macbeth has resolved to undergo cannot take place without the assistance of diabolical spirits. For the Elizabethan audience these proclamations were not mere rhetoric, but an actual conjuration of the infernal powers with whom Lady Macbeth is proposing to conclude a pact.[57] Pity and remorse, two primal forces in mankind, must be eliminated so that Lady Macbeth may perpetrate evil with unchecked cruelty. It is typical of Shakespeare that he presents psychic processes as being physical processes also, violently disturbing the human organism (in keeping with contemporary ideas). This is the reason for Lady Macbeth's demand:

> make thick my blood,
> Stop up th'access and passage to remorse;

(43–4)

The night too is summoned as an accomplice in the crime that must be covered up and hidden from sight:

> Come, thick Night,
> And pall thee in the dunnest smoke of Hell,
> That my keen knife see not the wound it makes,
> Nor Heaven peep through the blanket of the dark,
> To cry, 'Hold, hold!'   (50–4)

Night is to wrap itself in darkness as in a shroud. Dr Johnson deplored the vulgarity of the word 'blanket' ('an epithet now seldom heard but in the stable', *The Rambler*, no. 168), but for us the invocation is made particularly effective by the use of such everyday words which give 'unfamiliar horror a tangible quality'.[58] The occurrence of the word 'hell' confirms Lady Macbeth's awareness of the pact which she has concluded with the infernal powers, the 'murth'ring ministers' (48). Yet 'heaven' appears in the same sentence, and it is heaven rather than a human being that in Lady Macbeth's imagination discovers the murder, for it is from heaven that the cry 'Hold, hold!' rings out. With the visualization of the weapon ('my keen knife') these lines anticipate not only the deed, but also the fear of the murder being discovered and the murderer apprehended. Lady Macbeth knows, as does Macbeth during his first soliloquy, that there is judgement in heaven, but she represses this knowledge, whereas for Macbeth the divine powers take shape as 'heaven's Cherubins'. As will be apparent on several subsequent occasions, Lady Macbeth is less imaginative than her husband.

The cry 'Hold, hold!' brings the soliloquy to a close on a note of fear. Lady Macbeth is interrupted again, this time by another voice. Several times in *Macbeth* we hear calls and voices from afar. Our sense of hearing is appealed to, though sometimes indirectly, as often as our sense of sight. In these final lines both are combined. The hoarse croaking of the raven at the beginning of the soliloquy, signalling 'the fatal entrance of Duncan', is an instance of the contribution of sounds from the animal world to the 'acoustic underscoring' of the anxiety and foreboding of the action.

The attentive reader will be struck by the frequency with which this soliloquy points to past and future, inviting comparisons. Thus the last lines illustrate the continuing significance of the night: as background, as symbol, as active element. Even the invocations to the night invite comparison because they are indicative of the differences in character between the partners in crime and marriage. Macbeth's words are:

> Come, seeling Night,
> Scarf up the tender eye of pitiful Day,
>
> (III.ii.46–7)

and already in the first act:

> Stars, hide your fires!
> Let not light see my black and deep desires.
>
> (I.iv.50–1)

Why does Shakespeare choose a soliloquy to present the 'dehumanization' of Lady Macbeth at this particular point? Why this particular form? What does this signify for the scenes that follow? How does her yielding to evil compare with that of Macbeth? Macbeth's two great soliloquies will provide fresh opportunities for these questions to be asked, and, in part, answered.

MACBETH SHRINKS BACK FROM THE MURDER
I.vii.1–28

Hautboys and torches. Enter, and pass over the stage, a Sewer, and divers Servants with dishes and service. Then enter MACBETH.

Macb. If it were done, when 'tis done, then 'twere well
   It were done quickly: if th' assassination

Could trammel up the consequence, and catch
With his surcease success; that but this blow
Might be the be-all and the end-all—here,   5
But here, upon this bank and shoal of time,
We'd jump the life to come.—But in these cases,
We still have judgment here; that we but teach
Bloody instructions, which, being taught, return
To plague th' inventor: this even-handed Justice   10
Commends th' ingredience of our poison'd chalice
To our own lips. He's here in double trust:
First, as I am his kinsman and his subject,
Strong both against the deed; then, as his host,
Who should against his murtherer shut the door,   15
Not bear the knife myself. Besides, this Duncan
Hath borne his faculties so meek, hath been
So clear in his great office, that his virtues
Will plead like angels, trumpet-tongu'd, against
The deep damnation of his taking-off;   20
And Pity, like a naked new-born babe,
Striding the blast, or heaven's Cherubins, hors'd
Upon the sightless couriers of the air,
Shall blow the horrid deed in every eye,
That tears shall drown the wind.—I have no spur   25
To prick the sides of my intent, but only
Vaulting ambition, which o'erleaps itself
And falls on th' other—

The first thing that strikes us about the great soliloquy[59] is
its extraordinary range of successive, interrelated states of
consciousness and points of view. First we see Macbeth
brooding over his problems with an increasing awareness
of the unreality of his wishes. Then we listen as he assesses
his own situation with astonishing clarity, but at the same
time looks beyond it, debating briefly the question of what
the afterlife will bring. After an abrupt transition we
witness his succumbing to a vision of cosmic proportions

which overcomes him as he contemplates the crime that he is planning; the vision opens his eyes to the consequences of the regicide, and thus to his own guilt. Finally, in the last four lines, we see him consulting his conscience about his motives. These different ways of focusing on the future are matched by distinctive styles, and the abrupt transitions contribute to the impression of discontinuity which the whole soliloquy conveys.

Almost every line connects with what comes before and after, challenging the audience and reader time and again to compare what has already been seen and heard with what Macbeth is saying now; but several of his utterances also refer to matters that are unresolved or undecided in his own mind, thus giving rise to new questions. Beneath the surface of expressed thoughts there is a layer of unspoken meaning.

As with most of the soliloquies in the great tragedies the setting is significant. While Macbeth is speaking in the foreground, in the background the banquet in honour of the royal guest is being prepared, creating by its atmosphere of conviviality and hospitality a deeply ironic contrast.

For the first time Macbeth is alone on the stage. Although we have seen him in varying company and heard diverse assessments of his character, his first soliloquy comes relatively late so that we are eager to hear an answer to the question that has occurred to us on several occasions: will he carry out the deed or will he perhaps turn back even now? The soliloquy will provide no clear answer, and this contributes to its particular effect.

The soliloquy begins in the midst of Macbeth's deliberations. His words and deeds in the preceding scenes have made it clear that the thought of the murder (described when it first occurred to him as 'fantastical' I.i.139) continues to go round inside his head and will not let go of him. Thus the reference to the deed as 'it', the second word of the soliloquy, is not only a refusal to admit the wicked and unambiguous word 'murder', but also a sign of his continuing preoccupation with it. The shape and sounds of the first one and a half lines, with their repetitive sound patterns, already arouse our attention. Of the thirteen words twelve are monosyllables. The staccato tone with frequent strong stresses deviates from the regular pattern of the blank verse even more than in other passages. The shape of the verse even at the beginning of the soliloquy thus indicates that an insoluble problem has already been painfully considered, and that this is by no means the last word, however logical and rational it may sound. The following sentence, much the same in content, is very different in style, not only because of the complex Latinate vocabulary and unusual imagery, but also because of the puzzling syntax and the play on words, whereby the sequence 'surcease'–'success' includes a reference to the murder, for 'surcease' can be predicated both to Duncan and to 'consequence'. This indirect manner of speech is typical of Macbeth, who still clings to the hypothetical 'If it were done, when 'tis done' although the unreal conditional construction is in itself an indication that swift action does not necessarily mean action without consequences. Macbeth seeks to apply rational thought to the irrational.

The word 'done', one of the keywords of the play, which includes 'done with', 'finished' within its semantic field, occurs three times at the beginning of the soliloquy, thus marking the point round which Macbeth's thoughts revolve.[60] If no consequences were to be feared on earth then the deed could easily be carried out – this seems to be the basic thought behind these first lines. The murder is still not referred to explicitly in the second sentence, which contains a further unreal conditional construction, 'should trammel up the consequence'; and 'his' (Duncan's name is still not mentioned) death should stifle any repercussions. This idea is formulated in even more radical terms in the next sentence, with the coining of the two compounds 'be-all' and 'end-all'; the sentence ends with the readiness to 'jump the life to come'. The emphatic 'But here, upon this bank and shoal of time' betrays Macbeth's keen awareness of the time dimension, as of the life to come – however eager he may be to deny both. These seven lines, incomparable in their bold compactness, their expressiveness and their range of associations, reflect the inner condition of a man who knows that he must reject the fulfilment of the wishes that pass before his mind's eye; yet even as they pass they betray his familiarity with what it is that is being negated.

In the next lines there is a change of tone and rhythm. The constantly modified reasoning is replaced by an extraordinary clarity that extends so far that Macbeth is able to see himself as from a great distance. He knows that there is judgement here on earth. He sees justice appear even-handed before him, a surprising acknowledgement from one who has seemed to indulge in illusions. What he has to say about Duncan and about his obligations towards him makes his capacity for objective judgement and for recognition of the norms and order of the world even more plain. What has been formulated in abstract terms is now filled out with concrete detail. Macbeth knows that he is Duncan's 'host, / Who should against his murtherer shut the door, / Not bear the knife myself.' (14–16) The two implied gestures signal the events of the plot, and invite comparison with the last lines of Lady Macbeth's second soliloquy: 'That my keen knife see not the wound it makes' (I.v.52). We are provided with two different angles on the intended murder, each one indicative of the character of the speaker.

These moments of insight create the impression that Macbeth is already pronouncing the verdict on himself, and this impression is strengthened by the lines that follow. The description of Duncan's noble qualities leads without any break in syntax into the apocalyptic vision of the indictment for murder. Those very virtues displayed by Duncan

> Will plead like angels, trumpet-tongu'd, against
> The deep damnation of his taking-off;
> And Pity, like a naked new-born babe,
> Striding the blast, or heaven's Cherubins, hors'd
> Upon the sightless couriers of the air,
> Shall blow the horrid deed in every eye,
> That tears shall drown the wind. (19–25)

These lines, more than any others in the play, have been interpreted in diverse and controversial ways. Suffice it to say that Shakespeare cannot have intended there to be one unambiguous way of interpreting the juxtapositions, implications and images which almost exceed the bounds of the imagination in the monstrous vision which overwhelms Macbeth. Complex texts require complex responses.

Thus the reader or audience may be moved in a variety of ways by these lines. What strikes us as an unusual feature in the apocalyptic vision is the personification of pity as a tiny newborn child in the tumultuous skies; it is this, rather than vengeance and retribution which acts as the motive force of the world. Evil is confronted here not by yet more powerful avenging spirits but by an infant that is the weakest of all human beings and yet is endowed with the greatest cosmic power, sustained by the natural forces of the storm and able to achieve great things in the world. This is an image whose telling symbolism makes a deep impression on us, and is clearly influenced by the gospel story. No such figure could be found in pre-Shakespearean tragedies of revenge. The rapid succession of interwoven ideas leaves us almost breathless, and corresponds to Macbeth's state of mind as visionary seer: as in a dream images are amassed, conjoined and fused.[61] To search here for logical connections in the usual sense would probabl be inappropriate. The visualization of pity[62] is, incidentally, one of the many pieces of evidence that in Shakespeare's tragedies, however much the powers of evil may abound, there is always an awareness of goodness and positive values.

Macbeth is to become steeped in murder, but because he can speak in this way at this decisive moment he appears as one who can foresee the pity and mourning that Duncan's death will give rise to, and he recognizes the cruelty of the deed that he is planning. So this deed will by no means remain undiscovered and free of further consequences as Macbeth desired at the beginning of the soliloquy; it will shake the foundations of the world. We too are made to feel that the intended regicide is no ordinary murder but an act that will shatter the established order.[63]

The strength of Macbeth's imagination, so much greater than his wife's, has enabled him to travel far in space and time. The last three lines, however, bring a change in tone and tempo which is clearly discernible in every good production. Once more Macbeth considers himself and his intentions. His acknowledgement of the enormity of the deed has led him now to question his own motives. The answer raises new doubts, and there is a note of resignation in his retrenchment: 'I have no spur / To prick the sides of my intent, but only . . .' (25–6). Ambition is there, but evidently not in sufficient measure to justify such action. We recall the words spoken by Lady Macbeth in her first soliloquy: 'Thou . . . / Art not without ambition, but without / The illness should attend it' (I.v.18–20). Moreover, 'Vaulting ambition, which o'erleaps itself / And falls on th'other –' (27–8) will not lead reliably to success. The implied image of the rider who leaps so violently into the saddle that he falls down on the other side already anticipates failure.

The soliloquy breaks off in mid-sentence, interrupted by Lady Macbeth's entry, (though we can supply the missing word 'side'). Everything that has been said has some bearing on her as well, and Macbeth's most recent words exemplify one of the impediments on the path to the 'golden round' which she has referred to in her soliloquy (I.v). Now we are bound to wonder whether Macbeth will be able to advance any further towards the murder, after everything that we have heard. In his soliloquy he has spoken only of what could warn him and deter him. No convincing reasons for going forward could be found. Yet there must be some.

Between Macbeth's ability to see into the heart of things and his sinister drive to murder there is a deep abyss. Is he directed by supernatural powers? Is he acting from some inner compulsion? To what extent is he free to decide, able to choose between two different paths? This will remain in the background during the ensuing conversation with Lady Macbeth, but is nevertheless one of the fundamental questions posed by the tragedy as a whole.

MACBETH'S DAGGER SOLILOQUY

II.i.31–64

Macbeth. Go, bid thy mistress, when my drink is ready,
    She strike upon the bell. Get thee to bed.——
                                                    [*Exit Servant.*]

Is this a dagger, which I see before me,
The handle toward my hand? Come, let me clutch
    thee:——
I have thee not, and yet I see thee still.   35
Art thou not, fatal vision, sensible
To feeling, as to sight? or art thou but
A dagger of the mind, a false creation,
Proceeding from the heat-oppressed brain?
I see thee yet, in form as palpable   40
As this which now I draw.
Thou marshall'st me the way that I was going;
And such an instrument I was to use.——

Mine eyes are made the fools o' th' other senses,
Or else worth all the rest: I see thee still;   45
And on thy blade, and dudgeon, gouts of blood,
Which was not so before.—There's no such thing.
It is the bloody business which informs
Thus to mine eyes.—Now o'er the one half-world
Nature seems dead, and wicked dreams abuse   50
The curtain'd sleep: Witchcraft celebrates
Pale Hecate's off'rings; and wither'd Murther,
Alarum'd by his sentinel, the wolf,
Whose howl's his watch, thus with his stealthy pace,
With Tarquin's ravishing strides, towards his design 55
Moves like a ghost.—Thou sure and firm-set earth,
Hear not my steps, which way they walk, for fear
Thy very stones prate of my where-about,
And take the present horror from the time,
Which now suits with it.—Whiles I threat, he lives: 60
Words to the heat of deeds too cold breath gives.

                                        [*A bell rings.*]
I go, and it is done: the bell invites me.
Hear it not, Duncan; for it is a knell
That summons thee to Heaven, or to Hell.   [*Exit.*]

To fully understand Macbeth's second soliloquy, which
occurs in the next scene, we must recapitulate what has
happened in the meantime. In the dialogue which followed the first soliloquy Lady Macbeth has succeeded in
making Macbeth change his mind. At the beginning of the
dialogue he has said: 'We will proceed no further in this
business' (31), showing that the apocalyptic vision has
made him waver in his resolve, but at the end of the scene
we hear the opposite: 'I am settled' (80).

As is often the case in Shakespeare's tragedies, before the
decisive act there is an apparent easing of the suspense in a
scene where evasive and indirect communication replaces
'direct speech'. We know what motivates Macbeth and

what is imminent, but in the conversation with Banquo none of this reaches the surface. Macbeth skilfully evades Banquo's questions, at the same time feeling his way forward in order to find out what Banquo thinks. The scene is rich in irony and ambiguity, and is typical of a series of scenes in which Shakespeare exploits the phenomenon of discrepant awareness. When Macbeth is left alone on stage we wait for him to remove his mask and tell us what progress he and his murderous intent are making.

This soliloquy immediately precedes the murder and it is fundamentally different from the one in the last scene of the first act, both in form and in what it tells us of the inner experience of the speaker. In the first soliloquy Macbeth was overpowered by a vision which culminated in great clarity of perception, but in this soliloquy vision is replaced by hallucination. Macbeth's over-active imagination confronts him with his own evil intention, making him perceive himself and what he is about to do as in a mirror. There is no longer any question of retreat or wavering or qualms of conscience, even though his divided self is evident as he is torn between the chimera and the recognition that that is precisely what it is. The scope of the soliloquy has narrowed, the speaker does not see beyond his immediate surroundings; only towards the end is there a widening of perspective. Unlike the first soliloquy, this one involves a kind of dialogue throughout. The narrowing of perspective finds expression in the recurring focus on the 'partner', the dagger. Closer examination reveals that this very narrowing, together with other skilful techniques, causes fascinating effects. First, however, it is necessary to consider the stagecraft by which the soliloquy is fitted into the framework of suspense and expectation.

After the departure of Banquo and Fleance, the servant is sent off with instructions to let Lady Macbeth know that she should ring the bell when Macbeth's drink is ready. Thus the audience will keenly await the ringing of the bell expecting this to be the signal for the deed. The soliloquy is spoken during this time of waiting. It is therefore framed within a more specific time-span than the earlier soliloquies.

There is also more movement and gesture than in the earlier soliloquies, demanding that the actor should fully 'perform' his part.[64] Since the dagger as partner does not remain constant throughout, but is perceived by Macbeth in changing form, there are dramatic changes in language and intonation. This becomes apparent when we examine the different sections of the speech. It does not begin in a reflective vein but with the sight of something that stuns him. The opening question – whether what he sees before him is a dagger – is the cue to the whole soliloquy. He is confronted by a chimera but he does not at once recognize it as such. He tries to grasp the dagger, and cannot, yet still he sees it. Four times in the soliloquy he falters, undecided between acknowledging the 'reality' of the dagger and dismissing it as a phantom; clear recognition of the hallucination as a form of self-delusion alternates with yielding to it. Whether one sees in this uncertainty Macbeth's struggle with his warning conscience, a further instance of temptation, or a veering to and fro between illusion and reality will depend on the vantage-point of the observer. Whereas a modern audience will see in the dagger a psychological projection of Macbeth's desires, the Elizabethans would have seen it rather as a temptation put in his way by supernatural powers. They would have seen Macbeth as having been driven into a vicious circle by the witches' greetings, coerced into something from which he could not escape. Later eras, in keeping with altered views of the world, have accorded less significance to supernatural powers and ascribed to Macbeth a higher measure of free will. Shakespeare's great skill lies in presenting what happens to Macbeth in such a way that we are called upon ourselves to provide the ultimate answer, and to consider the manner in which the powers of evil can take possession of a human being.[65]

However, it was certainly also Shakespeare's intention to present to us a Macbeth tricked and deceived, not merely a victim of self-delusion. The vision of the dagger occurs in that same deceptive twilight in which the witches' scene took place. Macbeth suspects from the outset that he is being tricked; when he addresses the dagger for the second time he already calls it 'fatal vision' (36), and two lines further on he describes it as 'dagger of the mind', as 'false creation / Proceeding from the heat-oppressed brain'. In order to reassure himself that his senses are responding to reality he seizes his own dagger, which seems no more palpable than the one he sees before him (40/41). The drawing of the dagger is symbolic, for with it Macbeth will shortly carry out the murder. He knows that the dagger which he sees before him is not some indeterminate dagger, but the murder weapon (42/3), and he is in no doubt as to the import of the dagger's movement when it seems to show him the way to the scene of the murder (42). Yet when Macbeth says 'the way that I *was* going' he concedes that he had already taken his decision. We know that he will now follow the dagger irrevocably; the blood that he sees on blade and dudgeon are in incontrovertible anticipation of the bloody deed that is about to be carried out, although Macbeth recognizes here also the possibility that his 'eyes are made the fools o' th'other senses' (44). Hardly has the phantom finally vanished than Macbeth realizes quite clearly what has been happening: 'It is the bloody business which informs / Thus to mine eyes' (48). He knows that it is a foreshadowing or an embodiment of the intended murder. The word 'business', used both by Lady Macbeth and now by Macbeth to designate the murder, betrays cynicism, but also unwillingness to use the actual word, which does not occur until later in the soliloquy in the phrase 'wither'd Murther' (52).

The soliloquy, however, does not end with the disappearing of the imaginary dagger. From the confines within which Macbeth, as if spellbound, perceived only the instrument of death, his gaze now turns towards the nocturnal world outside. A new vision, this time of a quite different sort, arises. Macbeth's powerful imagination envisages the one half-world clothed in night, appearing, as it may well do to the murderer, to be a conspiracy of all dark and evil powers. Macbeth has a secret understanding with the demonic forces of witchcraft. It is of these that he now speaks, and it is with them that he is in league.

This finds expression in certain features of the language. Mention is made of 'wicked dreams' only, and they abuse sleep. Even Hecate, the mistress of the witches' coven who does not make her actual appearance until two later scenes (III.v and IV.i), is referred to in these lines. Macbeth cannot rid himself of the thought of the witches, however strongly he may have maintained to Banquo earlier in the scene 'I think not of them' (22). The whole soliloquy is a continuation of something which began when he first encountered them (I.iii).

Yet the second part of the soliloquy culminates in the personification of 'wither'd Murther' that Macbeth sees in his mind's eye. Hints of concrete features are combined with abstract notions, to evoke the image of murder alarmed by his sentinel the wolf, in anticipation of Macbeth's murderous deed. The 'stealthy pace' of murder, moving 'like a ghost' towards his goal, may be taken to represent Macbeth's own steps to which he makes direct reference three lines later. Moreover, in equating the 'stealthy pace' with Tarquin's 'ravishing strides' (55), Macbeth is admitting himself to be one who sets out to ravish innocence (compare Iachimo's soliloquy, *Cymbeline* II.ii.12–14). He projects his own intentions into self-conceived fantasies, making them into accomplices who incite him to carry out the deed. He observes himself as he draws closer to the murder. It is the most spine-chilling instance of one of Shakespeare's great accomplishments in this tragedy: to have the hero prefigure what he will do and how he will be affected by the deed.

The ease and assurance with which Shakespeare creates this sequence of heterogeneous images – dead nature, Hecate and the witches' coven, Tarquin, the howling wolf – and groups them around the spectral centrepiece of murder, reflects the intense and fast-moving sweep of Macbeth's imagination.

In the last six lines Macbeth speaks before he departs to do the deed there is a renewed narrowing of scope. He no longer addresses the unknown, the world of fantasy, but the solid earth that bears him. He calls it 'sure and firm-set', for it seems to sustain him against the invisible world of the imagination which has become overwhelming. He asks the earth not to hear his steps; the very stones might utter sounds and betray him. Then comes a phrase in which Macbeth expresses his appalling fear, giving himself away: 'the present horror' (59). He speaks like a man observing himself in a dream, talking about his steps as if they were separate from him. This splitting of himself, the capacity to confront himself like a stranger, was already noticeable in his speeches in the first act. It is in monologue that such self-duplication can be shown most convincingly.

The bell rings, bringing the soliloquy to a close. Six monosyllables encompass Macbeth's going and the performing of the deed, as if it were already done. The last two lines are addressed to one whose presence has been felt throughout the soliloquy although he has not been named until this moment: Duncan. Lady Macbeth, by contrast, has not been in Macbeth's thoughts during this soliloquy or the preceding one. The rhyming couplet at the end of the scene, and the rhyming of the lines prior to the ringing of the bell, follow a convention which Shakespeare observed in his great tragedies (compare, for instance, the end of Hamlet's soliloquies, II.ii.600–1; III.ii.389–90;

III.iii.97–8), but it also contributes at this point to a noticeable alteration in tone. Macbeth no longer speaks in profound fear and horror of the imminent murder, but almost with cynical assurance, as if he wanted to free himself now from the immense tension in order to proceed without delay to the 'bloody business' (48). Moreover, the final self-revealing note in the soliloquy, the macabre last word 'Hell' (64), goes against Macbeth's better knowledge. To suggest that Duncan might go to hell rather than to heaven contradicts everything that Macbeth himself has said about him in his first soliloquy.

Thus, shortly before the deed is done, the soliloquy focuses our attention once more on the sort of man Macbeth is, and the nature of his inner experience. The moral problem that is at issue here is not directly addressed, nor is the inner conflict clarified by means of abstract notions. On the contrary, the soliloquy is entirely removed from the sphere of abstract moral conflict, which has been transmuted into inner drama, which in turn finds expression in images and visions. The soliloquy has created not only its own form of interlocution, but also its own atmosphere and visionary dimensions, and it reveals a deep layer of Macbeth's personality while at the same time directing our eyes far into the distance.

Othello

OTHELLO'S FINAL SOLILOQUY
V.ii. 1–22

> DESDEMONA *in bed asleep.*
>
> *Enter* OTHELLO, *with a light.*

Oth. It is the cause, it is the cause, my soul,
    Let me not name it to you, you chaste stars:
    It is the cause, yet I'll not shed her blood,
    Nor scar that whiter skin of hers than snow,
    And smooth, as monumental alabaster: 5

Yet she must die, else she'll betray more men.
Put out the light, and then put out the light:
If I quench thee, thou flaming minister,
I can again thy former light restore,
Should I repent me; but once put out thine,   10
Thou cunning pattern of excelling nature,
I know not where is that Promethean heat
That can thy light relume: when I have pluck'd the
    rose,
I cannot give it vital growth again,
It must needs wither; I'll smell it on the tree,[*Kisses her.*
A balmy breath, that doth almost persuade   16
Justice herself to break her sword: once more:
Be thus, when thou art dead, and I will kill thee,
And love thee after: once more, and this the last,
So sweet was ne'er so fatal: I must weep,   20
But they are cruel tears; this sorrow's heavenly,
It strikes when it does love: she wakes.

There is renewed evidence in this soliloquy of Shakespeare's skill in providing and reinforcing meaningful links between the soliloquy and the situation in which it is set, so that what is seen on stage merges with what is seen in the mind's eye, both for the speaker and for the audience. But over and above this, in Othello's final soliloquy and in the exchange that follows between him and Desdemona when she awakes, the audience are under a hypnotic spell: Shakespeare creates a situation which fills us with troubled amazement and tense concern.[66]

The hero, unlike Iago, has only three soliloquies in the whole play and they do not occur until the second half. Othello is not characterized from the outset, as Brutus and Hamlet are, as a man naturally disposed towards reflection, self-analysis or introspection.[67] In the two earlier soliloquies (III.iii.262–83 and IV.ii.20–3) he reconsiders and reacts to what has just been said; the poisoning instigated by Iago is clearly demonstrated. Yet these soliloquies do not have the same power to illuminate the situation or the same devastating effect as the final soliloquy. Not until he begins to have doubts about his own identity does Othello turn to the soliloquy as a form of self-questioning.

There is an element of surprise in this last soliloquy, combined in a special way with careful preparation. In a sense the soliloquy also represents a *fermata* in the dramatic rhythm of the play, a slowing down of the rapid pace which has been set by the preceding scenes. The fact that most of the words (149 out of 169) are monosyllables contributes to this.[68] Yet ultimately the effectiveness of the soliloquy lies in the stark contrast between what Othello says and feels on the one hand, and the actual circumstances known to the audience on the other. There is a further contrast between the controlled and finely moulded language of the soliloquy, with its resonant and flowing lines, and the terrible inner turmoil beneath the surface. A man who is intent on murdering an innocent being speaks here in the guise of one who is performing a solemn rite. He assumes the dignity and the office of a judge – but of the executioner as well.

Unlike other tragedies, which have their subsidiary plots, digressions and complex network of actions, *Othello* is conceived in such a way that almost every moment fills us with expectations and suspense as to what will happen next. Time and again we ask, in hope or in fear, what is going to occur. When Othello, late at night, enters the chamber where Desdemona lies sleeping on her marriage-bed, the audience expect that the intended murder will now be carried out. We have been prepared for this by Othello's drastic avowals: 'I'll tear her all to pieces' (III.iii.438); 'I will chop her into messes' (IV.i.196); 'Thy bed, lust-stain'd, shall with lust's blood be spotted' (V.i.36).[69] In the same scenes we have witnessed the collapse of Othello's world and of his inner security, which was grounded in his love for Desdemona. In a moment of premonition he had expressed his fears 'And when I love thee not, / Chaos is come again' (III.iii.92–3). This chaos has now supervened. Desdemona's presumed unfaithfulness has unleashed uncontrollable passions and brutal thoughts of vengeance in Othello, driving him close to delirium. Seldom has Shakespeare presented so radical a change of personality within the space of two acts: in the first acts Othello excelled in imperturbable dignity and a self-control now lost; he has been overpowered in the meantime by ungovernable wildness and debasing thoughts and feelings.

So this is what we are expecting as Othello approaches the sleeping Desdemona; but our expectations are thwarted. Othello enters with unusual self-discipline. He seems to have regained the stately calm and with it the rich poetry which was characteristic of him during the first Acts. We are captivated once again by <u>euphony</u>, whereas in the preceding scenes his language had fallen apart and, instead of well-formed verses, we heard disconnected and explosive fragments and exclamations[70]; but it will not be long before Othello loses all control again, and this makes the soliloquy become a moment of quietness, though full of tensions, a holding back between two outbursts of violent excess. For the time being what we see and hear puts us in mind of the noble Moor of the first two Acts. We are filled with amazement and awe,[71] but even more with apprehension, as we experience this moment of calm before the storm.

The spectacle is one of incomparable symbolic force. Othello stands, torch in hand, beside his own marriage-bed, on which Desdemona lies sleeping – a picture of unblemished beauty, of tranquillity, under the protection of the night. The observer is aware of the profoundly paradoxical nature of what he sees before him. He is made conscious once more of the rare, exquisite and fragile quality of the unparalleled love of Othello and Desdemona. Yet Othello is in the process of destroying it irrevocably, has indeed already destroyed it within himself, while Desdemona has remained unaltered, not withdrawing from her husband in spite of the cruel wrong inflicted on her in the preceding Act, when Othello struck her and insulted her in the presence of the emissaries from Venice (IV.i.235; 239–41). She is still prepared to turn to him, his 'true and loyal wife' (IV.ii.35). One small step would suffice for the monstrous delusion to which Othello has succumbed to be recognized and revealed in time, and everything would be just as it was before. The audience may feel this for a moment, and yet know at the same time that it is precisely this possible turn of events which is in fact impossible. We perceive the terribly irony of the evident closeness of two people who are yet separated by an abyss of misunderstandings, contaminating poison and self-delusion. Thus the soliloquy, in this situation of a reconciliation which is still possible and yet impossible, is, among other things, an expression of the inner isolation into which Othello has passed.

As in earlier soliloquies, the significance and the symbolic power of the situation are enhanced by gesture and by stage properties. Othello addresses the light[72] that he holds in his hand as the symbol of the flame of life that must be quenched for ever when it is put out, though the candle can be lit again. At the same time his eyes, which, unlike his mind, can see things as they really are, light on Desdemona as she sleeps; her beauty overwhelms him once more so that he bends down to kiss her. The audience are reminded of the first kiss that the lovers exchanged (II.i.198). The reminiscence[73] is a poignant indication of what has changed in the meantime. The profound emotion that now breaks through Othello's strict self-discipline, moving him to tears, affects the audience too and brings home to us the agonized rift in the situation. Othello has forced himself into a role, but at this point the mask slips.

Our starting point in this discussion was Othello's entry, the setting of the scene, gestures and movements, symbolic stage-properties, and the alteration in tone. Consideration of the text, although no less important, was deferred. In this way we were able to see to what an extent the special effect of the soliloquy emanates from elements which do not demand a complete or precise understanding of the text.

The overall impression that we have gained is substantiated[74] when we look closely at single utterances, at imagery and phrasing; and yet at the same time new questions and contradictions arise. The diversity of interpretations accorded to this soliloquy – to the opening sentences alone – provides new evidence of a particular characteristic of Shakespeare's dramatic art: even in a soliloquy such as this, constructed on logical premises and reinforced by elevated rhetoric, we are in some doubt as to how exactly the text is to be understood.[75] Is this majestic self-justification a pose, or are we seeing once more the unbroken self that Othello presented to us in the first Acts? Does the language merely veil the chaos that is seething still beneath the surface? Does not Othello's shocking self-delusion border on presumptuous arrogance? Is not the threefold reference to the cause at the beginning of the soliloquy (a cause which remains unnamed) a revealing attempt to present the personal murder as an impersonal sacrifice offered to the world at large, an act of justice to which Othello feels himself summoned by a higher, even divine, duty, in order to prevent others from being harmed ('else she'll betray more men . . .' [6])? Likewise Brutus had attempted to present Caesar's murder as a judicial rite ('Let's be sacrificers, but not butchers, Caius' [II.i.166]); but whereas the words with which Brutus began his soliloquy were unambiguous ('It must be by his death' [II.i.10]), Othello's opening 'It is the cause . . .' (1) leaves room for speculation.[76] Do not the 'chaste stars' which Othello calls to witness, unwilling as he is to call adultery by its name, involve a further presumptuous attempt to elevate the murder to the plane of purifying atonement? There is no mention now of vengeance, although the audience will not have forgotten the oath of vengeance sworn in the third act (III.iii.438, 450). On the other hand, it has frequently been noted that with reference to Othello's language it is problematic to speak of a surface beneath which other matters are concealed, since Othello responds with single-minded intensity just as the occasion demands; the absolute openness of his character, which admits no half-measures and no self-doubt, is at once his strength and his weakness.

These reservations are justified but they are not sufficient to appease the audience, who will sense that the gap between Othello's words and what they themselves know and see before them can hardly be bridged. In all probability this impression is just what Shakespeare intended. We are all the more disturbed by the terrifying contradictions when Othello eloquently praises Desdemona's beauty as she lies asleep before him (4–5), and in the same breath affirms that he will shed no blood but that she must die notwithstanding, and then, a few lines further on, speaks of her as the rose (13–14) whose scent, equated with her 'balmy breath' (16), beguiles him. Thus in the throes of monstrous self-delusion Othello is still in touch with the reality of the senses. Indeed, his sensuous evocation of Desdemona's beauty – from the comparison of her skin to snow and alabaster up to the unforgettable image of the rose – enables us also to contemplate her as she sleeps. He is deeply moved, indeed overwhelmed, by Desdemona's loveliness, and this is expressed by his actions as well as by his words; at the same time it is clear to him that the quenching of her vital flame will be irreversible, and he is almost moved to lay aside the 'sword of justice'.

This 'almost', that Shakespeare often allows to intrude for a moment just before the point of no return at the climax of his tragedies, lasts only for a moment; it is already rejected in the next line. We note that this soliloquy, like others, does not have one clear line of development leading from beginning to end, but rather a broken inner thread. This emerges most clearly in the last seven lines, which cause us to question in retrospect the firm self-assurance and sovereignty of the opening lines. We realize that these are the words of a wounded soul suffering in agony. The soliloquy moves us deeply and sets every nerve on edge. The suspense is increased by our awareness of the irrevocable running out of time as we watch and hear.

This is a great moment in the Othello music, that unmistakable lyric poetry whose solemn resonance and rhythm have marked Othello's speech since his first appearance, elevating him above the level of the other characters in the play. Yet this blend of the exotic and the extravagant with majestic and self-conscious dignity has also caused him to become isolated from the others who interact around him. He has no access to the easy give and take of conversation, has in fact for some time been incapable of dialogue, as the ensuing exchange of words tragically demonstrates. Everything that he says (except in the scenes of despair in the fourth Act) is weighty, and has a loftiness that makes us listen most attentively when he begins to speak. Some have seen in this an element of bombast, of self-projection sustained by excessive self-aggrandizement,[77] but in reply one may say that this style is appropriate to the monstrous self-delusion to which Othello has succumbed. Exaggerated self-esteem and the readiness to be deceived have always been close neighbours. Looked at in this way, the language of the soliloquy becomes less difficult to understand.

The distinctive music of Othello's speech, in this soliloquy in particular, has been examined with great expertise. The language has been found to be 'high-coloured, rich in sound and phrase, stately. Each word solidifies as it takes its place in the pattern.'[78] The images appeal not only to our sense of sight but also of touch and smell. The human sphere is closely linked with the infinity of the nocturnal cosmos, the figurative detail of the near-at-hand with the elaborate and far-reaching symbol. After simple and direct observation may come a single word of striking brilliance.

It is true of this soliloquy as of many others that it expresses what is felt and seen as well as what is thought. Moreover, some thoughts only are expressed while others are held back. The candescent imagery of these lines does not serve to clarify abstract thought; rather it is sense perception transmuted into verse. A distinction between thought and perception had not as yet been made. In all the great poets of the time, but especially in Shakespeare, we find in the language an interpenetration of thinking and feeling, of abstraction and contemplation, of rational analysis and fantasy. Modern concepts divide into two separate spheres elements that for Shakespeare were still blended. We can describe the abundant appeal to the senses displayed in Shakespeare's soliloquies, the precise focus on descriptive detail, the strongly pictorial quality, but this is only one side of the phenomenon as a whole, for which we have no word because we live in a time that has lost sight of such wholeness.

King Lear

LEAR'S SOLILOQUIZING SPEECHES

When we call *King Lear* to mind, it may at first seem that in this play the tragic hero is particularly given to the soliloquy, but when we look more closely we see that it is less a matter of soliloquies than of soliloquizing speeches, which, like the asides, are very close to the soliloquy. Lear's great colloquy with the raging elements (III.ii), and also his visions of the world's injustice (IV.vi) – to mention only two of the speeches that occur to us when we are prompted to think of his soliloquies – are strictly speaking not soliloquies because Lear is not alone on the stage, but surrounded throughout by people who are listening. Nevertheless, such speeches, which from the third Act onwards become the prevalent and characteristic form of utterance spoken by the ousted king, are soliloquies in a more profound sense than are the blatant self-expositions of Edgar and Edmund. Lear's soliloquizing speeches are the natural form of expression of a man driven into the isolation of insanity.

In earlier plays there have been hints of something that is now exploited to the full: it is as if Shakespeare were making free with the opportunity the soliloquy provides to reproduce in speech what has not yet been filtered and ordered by a consciousness disciplined to consider the requirements of dialogue with another person. In the first Act we can already discern a break in the thread of communication,[79] for in the fourth scene it is clear that the exchange is no longer restricted to the rational level, to the give and take of question and answer. Lear does not always respond to Goneril's remarks, any more than to the interjections of the Fool. We witness him working out his thoughts laboriously; we listen as he invokes Nature's help and levels charges against himself while insight begins to dawn and fragments of past memories rise to the surface. His questions are no longer directed to a specific person; oaths, accusations, outbursts of anger, exclamations follow one another in rapid succession.[80] To the same degree that Lear disengages himself from 'interlocution', the soliloquizing speech develops. Beside him stands the Fool, whose utterances display a similar tendency to become detached from any specific counterfigure, though obviously for quite different reasons. The Fool's comments and witty comparisons, his apt tales and his snatches of traditional songs are soliloquizing speeches spoken to the world at large, but whereas the audience are in a sense invited to become involved and to listen, the situation is very different with Lear's self-forgetting and yet egocentric utterances – he scarcely seems to be aware any longer of anyone around him. What he says erupts from within and exposes unsparingly his state of mind and spirit. For entire scenes and Acts the talking-at-cross-purposes of the two characters who have moved along such different paths in the direction of the soliloquy becomes the most typical form of speech. The powerful words which Lear hurls at the raging elements in the first scene on the heath (III.ii), apostrophizing, challenging and conjuring them, are a first climax of this type of speech.

Only in the second part of the scene does Lear, who is now close to madness, turn to his companion, the Fool, who interrupts him several times. In the earlier part of the scene his words are addressed to the elements, to lightning, hurricane and thunder. With this powerful verse Lear evokes the sense of the storm raging around him and fills the empty space with violent images of a monstrous turmoil in Nature. At the same time he makes manifest the storm within himself, each storm matching and pervading the other.[81] What was formerly described as creation of atmosphere is now given a much wider significance, for this tragedy is not enacted solely on the human level. The elements are involved also; the whole cosmos takes part in the action, reflecting human activities on a larger scale.

LEAR'S VISIONS

IV.vi.151–75

Lear. What! art mad? A man may see how this world goes with no eyes. Look with thine ears: see how yond justice rails upon yond simple thief. Hark, in thine ear: change places, and, handy-dandy, which is the justice, which is the thief? Thou hast seen a farmer's dog bark at a beggar?

Glou. Ay, Sir.
Lear. And the creature run from the cur? There
    thou might'st behold
  The great image of Authority: 160
  A dog's obey'd in office.
  Thou rascal beadle, hold thy bloody hand!
  Why dost thou lash that whore? Strip thine own
    back;
  Thou hotly lusts to use her in that kind
  For which thou whipp'st her. The usurer hangs
    the cozener.   165
  Thorough tatter'd clothes small vices do appear;
  Robes and furr'd gowns hide all. Plate sin with gold,
  And the strong lance of justice hurtless breaks;
  Arm it in rags, a pigmy's straw does pierce it.   169
  None does offend, none, I say, none; I'll able 'em:
  Take that of me, my friend, who have the power
  To seal th' accuser's lips. Get thee glass eyes;
  And, like a scurvy politician, seem
  To see the things thou dost not. Now, now, now,
    now;
  Pull off my boots; harder, harder; so.   175

In the fourth Act (IV.vi) the king appears in his madness
on the coast near Dover, accompanied by Gloucester and
Edgar. In his soliloquizing speeches Lear depicts a series of
scenes of injustice and hypocrisy, assumed grandeur and
wrongful punishment. These images arise before his mind's
eye, detached from the action of the play and not suggested
directly by the words of the blinded Gloucester, whose part
in the dialogue is more passive. Time seems to stand still as
the mad king receives these visions. The action moves from
without to within, and our attention is riveted to what is
taking place in Lear himself. The closely observed sym-
bolical situations in which Lear discerns the reversals and
paradoxes of the world are at the same time insights, and

represent a step forward on the path that Lear must follow. His own suffering has brought him closer not only to sympathy for the sufferings of others, but also to an understanding of all things human. Thus these soliloquizing speeches, in which the multilayered themes of the whole play are reiterated,[82] contain a new view of the world which challenges previously accepted values. Madness has exposed a deeper level of awareness in Lear, freeing him from the fictitious values that have encumbered his previous grasp of the affairs of the world. It is significant that the images which Lear uses at this point circle round the central theme of appearance and reality (167, 173–4), for Lear's gaze now penetrates beneath the surface of the apparent and mendacious, the spurious and conventional. Now that the directing of events has been taken out of his hands and he has been forced into a purely passive role, the spirit of scrutiny becomes active in him.

The figure of the dog from whom the beggar runs is described by Lear himself as 'the great image of Authority', while the visions of the rascal beadle, the usurer and the 'strong lance of justice' have to do with the aforesaid notions of wrongful punishment and the innocent sinner, of apparent and real guilt. In the tragedies the inner substance of the action is often reflected in metaphor, and in remarks and observations which seem to be made in a quite different connection; the same subject appears refracted in various ways, with varying degrees of intensity. Just as Lear and Gloucester, Regan and Goneril, Edmund and Cornwall see themselves as judges and arrogate the role of judge, so also they are called before the court themselves. The mad Lear in the hovel on the heath stages legal proceedings against his absent daughters who are represented by stools, for variations on the theme of justice preoccupy him. In these speeches, however, this theme undergoes an amazing metamorphosis. Lear in his madness can put into words what would hardly be credible if it was spoken by a man in his senses ('None does offend, none, I say none' [170]), and we ourselves find it difficult to accept, so that one critic justly comments: 'The anarchic ultimate of the last line marks the furthest point in Lear's "understanding"'.[83]

Much of this speech, as of most of Lear's other soliloquizing speeches, is in the form of direct address. Lear sees the accused, the false judges, the virtuous-seeming great ones of this world, just as earlier or in the mock trial scene in the hovel on the heath he thought he saw his daughters before him, and addressed them as if they were there; but in these deranged speeches Lear is actually addressing not only the figures of his visions but beyond them the whole of mankind. When he speaks to blind Gloucester he really means to address all human beings, with whom he wants to share the knowledge that he has gained.[84] Thus in *King Lear* both direct address of a figure present in the imagination and the direct address of the audience, characteristic of pre-Shakespearean soliloquies, have been extended to an extraordinary degree, but here the limit is reached which this type of utterance may not exceed. In *King Lear* Shakespeare has hazarded something which surpasses the accepted bounds of drama. The speeches of the mad king are an example of this expanding force, which makes it possible for the tragedy to be playing on several different arenas at the same time.

These speeches of Lear's are also the exception in the play. When we examine the soliloquies of Edgar and Edmund we realize that Shakespeare still retains the conventional use of the soliloquy, exploiting it as a dramatic means of self-presentation and justification, and of conveying information to the audience. Even the late romances continue to provide numerous examples of soliloquies in which the speaker rather crudely sets forth his intentions, or gives exposition lacking in psychological credibility, or commentary without regard to consistency of characterization. Whenever Shakespeare could find a use for such relicts of popular theatre he absorbed them into his plays, which do not lose any of their effectiveness in the process. His art is all-embracing and many-faceted, it can assimilate everything and make something out of anything, whether it is a simple motif, an unsophisticated stage device or the most incredible of events. He seizes on the extraordinary and the daring, but he also returns to what has been well-established and frequently repeated. In Shakespeare's soliloquies, as elsewhere in his plays, the most disparate elements are brought together, to be transformed 'into something rich and strange'.

5
Conclusion

Having looked at a selection of soliloquies, let us now try to summarize what it is that constitutes the originality of this aspect of Shakespeare's art. Are there recurrent characteristics more representative of Shakespeare than of other dramatists? In providing an answer to this question we resume the discussion of some matters raised briefly in the introduction.

Our observations do not, of course, apply to all of Shakespeare's soliloquies. Wherever it seems expedient, Shakespeare continues to make use of the traditional conventions of the soliloquy, letting characters introduce themselves, convey information, provide an exposition or reveal plans.[1] Such soliloquies, which are still found at times even in the great tragedies,[2] are monolayered; they fulfil a limited purpose inconspicuously at the appropriate moment, so that the idea of regarding them as artless would not occur to the non-specialist – unless there were some reason to compare them systematically with those other soliloquies which have provided the material for the main chapters of this book, and which may indeed be considered under the heading 'the art of the soliloquy'.

In the introduction mention was made of several problems which have always presented themselves to the dramatist with regard to the soliloquy. How does Shakespeare succeed none the less in making most of his soliloquies so credible? This question, which really needs to be posed anew for each soliloquy, provides a key to the recognition of some fundamental elements of Shakespeare's art. For time and again we have the impression that the soliloquy has arisen naturally at this particular moment as the inevitable form of speech.[3] Closer examination usually reveals that Shakespeare has been preparing us carefully though unobtrusively for this moment of solitude. This can happen in various ways: through stagecraft preparing us for the character's solitude; or through words that make the necessity or the wish for solitude explicit. On some occasions the puzzling behaviour of a character may suggest that as soon as he or she is alone, the cause of this strangeness will be revealed. Sometimes Shakespeare makes a point of heightening the audience's curiosity about this figure. We feel that answers to questions which we would have liked to ask in the preceding scenes are now due.

The setting, too, can contribute to the credibility of the soliloquy. Often it is the night-time, together with sleeplessness, brooding restlessness or tense anticipation of what is to come, that provides the background for the solitary speech, and in most cases the night is not just a background, but is addressed as a participating and assisting agent. There are many other types of situation, particularly in the comedies and romances, which naturally give rise to the abandonment or isolation of a character: imprisonment, losing one's way, concealment. Other dramatists have exploited such situations, sometimes under Shakespeare's influence, but what is so distinctive of his art is the blend of stagecraft with other effects, whereby the audience is attuned to the soliloquy on several different levels at the same time.[4]

Here we must note above all the 'soliloquizing' disposition of certain characters. It is not by chance that the most significant soliloquies in the tragedies are spoken by Hamlet and Macbeth, in whom inner loneliness is combined with the compulsion to conceal their thoughts from those around them. Much the same can be said of Brutus and Lear.[5]

We are struck time and again by the appeal which the language of the soliloquies makes to our senses. A Shakespearean soliloquy makes us hear, see and feel. Almost every one includes concrete details and draws on observations from everyday life and nature, often in the most down-to-earth and palpable form. Even when the soliloquy is largely a vehicle for reflection, for intense consideration of a pending decision, it is not couched in abstract conceptual language, but in that psychophysical blend of the abstract and the concrete which is so particularly characteristic of Shakespeare.

Through the evocation of sense impressions the outside world continually invades the soliloquies – a further characteristic of Shakespeare's art. The inner vision is closely linked with the outer. The soliloquies do not take place on a separate plane of intellectual debate, they are directly related to the living world, though the time reference may be to present, past or future. Often the world of the speaker and the other characters, those who are for him and those who are against him, are reflected, and graphic instances of their various activities are recorded. Often an event that has happened before is reflected in the monologue, and its importance stressed. Our own observations are supplemented by a further perspective which enhances and increases our perceptions.

We see with the speaker's eyes so that we discern more clearly what is to be seen on the stage; and our imaginations are stimulated to visualize something that the speaker can see although it is hardly visible to us (as, for example, the sleeping Desdemona described by Othello,

V.ii.1–22, or the sleeping Imogen described by Iachimo in *Cymbeline* II.ii.14 ff). The soliloquy may create a picture of the setting, the locality with everything that belongs to it (as in *Romeo and Juliet* [II.ii.2 ff] or in *Cymbeline* [II.ii.11]), a tableau which contains its own significance; but sometimes the gaze of the speaker passes beyond the immediate surroundings, his imagination quickens and reaches out to the heavens or to a far country that takes shape before the inner eye. Even when the speaker looks into the past or into the future, the soliloquy unfolds in the here and now.

In pre-Shakespearean drama, as also in the plays of classical antiquity, in Seneca and in the medieval mystery plays, it had already become apparent that an imaginary partner was required for the soliloquy to come alive. Various forms of address, apostrophe and the use of fictitious dialogue within the soliloquy may be observed. Shakespeare took the development of dialogue within the monologue much further; and those who followed after him could not extend the multiplicity of partner situations that he devised. The speaker may address his ego, his own heart, or heavenly and earthly powers, or people absent, or sometimes even those present (but out of earshot); or he may address personifications, sun, moon and stars, real or imaginary objects (such as the dagger in *Macbeth*). The dialogue within the monologue is sustained by the interplay of questions and answers. A particular kind of dramatic effect arises when the soliloquy represents a process of transformation, of reversal, when the to and fro of question and answer results in a final attitude quite different from that prevailing at the beginning of the speech. Within the confines of such soliloquies a self-contained drama is played out. Shakespeare recognized more clearly than his contemporaries, and more clearly than most of his successors, that man is a paradoxical creature; this is apparent in many of the soliloquies.

The dramatic quality of the soliloquies is most evident in

the skilfully imparted hints on how the speech should be spoken and acted. As a man of the theatre Shakespeare quite clearly wrote the soliloquies with an eye to their performance; the texts include veiled or even direct indications of gestures, movements, facial expressions, sometimes of stage directions which lead to the playing out of a whole scene within the soliloquy, or which initiate a whole train of events. This development is already in evidence in the early plays, as is shown by the scene with Launce and his dog from *Two Gentlemen of Verona*. With such entertaining monologues, designed to be acted out as a complete scene before the audience (far removed from the lonely introspection of some soliloquies), Shakespeare was continuing a popular tradition,[6] but here, too, he ventured on new ground by combining the merry play-acting with self-revelation.

Implicit stage directions can be found at many points in Shakespeare's plays,[7] but in the soliloquies, where there is no dialogue partner, they are of particular importance. If one examines the usage of nineteenth- and twentieth-century dramatists in this respect one finds that as a rule there are extensive separate stage directions; in Shakespeare the guidelines for the actors are to be found in the text.

Moreover this text displays a striking range of stylistic creativity. Early on Shakespeare transcended the regularly patterned rhetoric of the tragedy of his predecessors,[8] influenced by Seneca; he found a style capable of amazing modulations, that could be adapted to the changing thoughts and feelings of the characters, with varying transitions and startling contrasts of mood. Or rather, these moods are suggested by the rhythm of the language as well as by the meanings of the words.

The wide range of style and language is of course a general characteristic of Shakespeare's plays, but in the soliloquies, particularly in those of the late tragedies, this variety is compressed into a small space. From this compactness there arises a sense of urgent spontaneity in the soliloquies, as if they were emerging by necessity from the consciousness of the speaker. In order to channel such an overflow of emotion directly into language, Shakespeare tends to let disjointed phrases take the place of well-formed sentences, often interrupting the flow of words and causing perceptible changes in tempo. This matches the dislocation of the train of thought observable in the great soliloquies of the tragedies. Shakespeare had realized early on that the thoughts of a man talking to himself do not follow one another in an ordered and logical sequence; they rise to the surface fragmented, and sometimes interspersed with other associations. Whereas in French tragedy, in Corneille and Racine, and in the earlier Senecan tragedy, we find soliloquies with well-ordered trains of thought, Shakespeare presents logical argumentation and ordered deliberation only when the situation demands it. In the soliloquies of the early and middle period there are more examples of such order. Later, reflection and emotion are intertwined to such an extent that the presentation of well-formed thought sequences becomes intermittent; often we must guess at the connections.[9]

It is above all this interconnection of thought and feeling, aptly matched by unusual diction, that characterizes Shakespeare's art in the soliloquies of the great tragedies. The language permeated with synaesthetic imagery makes it possible for thoughts to be felt and for feelings to be transformed at lightning speed into thoughts; it contributes to the simultaneous articulation of thinking and feeling, as does the bold phrasing which often disregards the rules of syntax and grammar (in which respect the language of the day was of course more flexible than ours). And occasionally in the late tragedies, as we see a character fall silent during a soliloquy, we witness a transition to speechlessness because language is no longer adequate for the expression of the emotions that overcome him at this moment.[10]

This is a far cry from the ordered syntactical and intellectual structures which prevailed with few exceptions in the soliloquies of Elizabethan drama; far also from the assumption still valid in Shakespeare's early soliloquies that everything could be put into words and made manifest by language. Increasingly Shakespeare replaces elucidation, originally one of the basic aims of the soliloquy, by half-tacit suggestion. Only when roles and situations demand it do we find elucidation as a prominent feature of the soliloquy.

In comparison with soliloquies by other dramatists of his own time, but also with those of the later seventeenth and eighteenth centuries, some of Shakespeare's achievements in the great tragedies seem to anticipate much later attempts to restore life to the soliloquy, and on occasion – as happens in some modern British plays – to replace words by silences.[11]

The effectiveness of some soliloquies may be attributed in part to the awareness of time imparted to the listener. Time is already used to good effect in Shakespeare's early plays; in the tragedies it becomes an element of dramatic art, exploited in different ways and on different levels. Early chapters have attempted to demonstrate this variety. A particular effect is created when the audience is tensely waiting, while the soliloquy is being spoken, for something to happen at any moment. Sometimes it is the speaker himself who conveys this sense of anticipation to the audience; examples that spring to mind occur in Macbeth's dagger soliloquy (II.i.33 ff), in Othello's soliloquy at the bedside of the sleeping Desdemona (V.ii.1 ff) and – in a quite different way – in Iachimo's soliloquy before the sleeping Imogen's bed (*Cymbeline* II.ii.11 ff). In each case there is an exciting, even sensational situation, within which the revelations of the soliloquy take place, sometimes transporting the audience to distant regions. Time can also be experienced in quite different ways. Now and then it seems to stand still, yielding in the audience's awareness to a far more rapid pace when the soliloquy is over and the action is resumed. At times the soliloquy looks backwards and forwards, linking past and future with one another,[12] allowing the time-span to extend far beyond the present in our imagination.

In pre-Shakespearean drama the soliloquy could already be an invitation not only to self-interrogation but also to observation of the surroundings. A recurrent type of soliloquy is the survey of the situation; the dramatist could use it to insert epic material, to include narrative and other kinds of information, which could not be presented adequately in the dialogue. Short soliloquies with the primary function of providing information, are frequently found in Shakespeare's plays, even in the tragedies. A closer look at his great soliloquies, however, shows us that everything that helps to convey information, local colour and background is so interwoven with the feelings and personality of the speaker that often we scarcely notice how we have been incidentally provided with details necessary to our understanding of the action. The survey of the situation is given a subjective quality.

Almost always the soliloquy results in a new or altered perspective; we view what follows, and sometimes review what has gone before, in a different light. This change in perspective is a technique frequently used by later dramatists, but it would appear that in the sixteenth and the seventeenth centuries no one else made use of it with such consistency and in such a variety of ways as Shakespeare.[13] Often there are several perspectives at the same time, joining and crossing so that several ways of assessing the action and the characters are open to the audience. The ambivalent image of several of Shakespeare's tragic heroes, and also of some of the characters in the comedies, has to do with this changing perspective, to which the soliloquies make a decisive contribution.

One of the basic functions of the soliloquy before Shakespeare's time was to admit the audience to plans and purposes previously unknown. In this way certain expectations are aroused, with which the events of the following scenes are then observed. Shakespeare took over this basic scheme, interweaving it with complex patterns of behaviour and psychologically determined reactions. We are constantly being required to revise our assessment of what has taken place, while new expectations are added to those that we already have. It often happens too, in the great tragedies and in the comedies of the middle years, that we ask ourselves whether the sentiments expressed in the soliloquies are authentic, or whether they are perhaps an exaggeration, a wrong reaction or even intentionally misleading.

This aspect of the soliloquies above all draws our attention to the phenomenon of the manipulation of audience response.[14] Certain characters seem to impart more of their true being in soliloquy than in dialogue. They provoke a response which oscillates between sympathy, withdrawal and doubt. This is the case, for instance, with Brutus, Hamlet, Macbeth, Iago and Othello.

By means of the soliloquy the audience, and the reader, are made to feel that they are being taken into the speaker's confidence. Not only are they given a glimpse of what is going on inside that character, they also learn things as yet unknown to the other characters. Thus they are given a certain superiority, and can feel one step ahead of the other characters in the play. There are many degrees of privy knowledge, of initiation into secrets, amongst the players as well as between one or more of them and the audience, with resulting discrepancies of awareness.[15] A great number of scenes, particularly in the comedies, derive the sense of suspense conveyed to the audience from this differentiation of shared knowledge. The soliloquies are important in this connection; they play a key part in letting us into a secret, or in giving us one-sided or even false information. We tend to listen more attentively when a soliloquy is delivered, for when a speaker is alone with us we believe that we will hear the truth.[16] On the other hand, it sometimes happens that we already have knowledge which goes beyond what is said in the soliloquy, or which even contradicts it. As a rule the objective value of a soliloquy can only be assessed at the end of the play.

If one looks at Shakespeare's soliloquies from this angle it becomes clear that they fulfil an important function with regard to the changing awareness of the audience, through changes in perspective, through the measure of shared knowledge, through the manipulation of audience response or through the constantly renewed challenge to the audience to question both themselves and the figure that is confronting them.

In the plays which contain several soliloquies by the same character, such as *Hamlet* and *Macbeth*, these speeches contribute in a particular way to the development of dramatic rhythm. Whenever the character is once more alone on the stage, embarking on a solitary speech, the audience recalls the similar situations that have gone before. Yet although the situation may appear to be the same, there has been an inner change. Looking back prompts the audience to make comparisons, to perceive changes that have arisen in the meantime. Between successive soliloquies a link is formed, prompting the audience to make comparisons by offering a sequence of portrayals of the same character under changing conditions. Some of the earlier chapters have attempted to show the extent to which Shakespeare made use of the potential resulting from this dramatic rhythm.

It is also profitable to ask at what point in the rhythmical progression of the play a soliloquy occurs, for there is no play in which the action proceeds uninterrupted at a constant tempo. There are moments when we pause for breath, moments for reflecting and reviewing the situation, and also moments when pent-up emotions erupt and find an outlet. The soliloquy allowed Shakespeare, as Una Ellis-Fermor phrased it, 'to let down a shaft of light into the hidden workings of the mind, to enable us to overhear its unspoken thought without in effect suspending the outward movement of the action or breaking the impression of the immediacy and reality of the dramatic world'.[17] When we listen to one of the great soliloquies it is as if we are being given access to a different plane, a new dimension. The soliloquy invariably creates a caesura, and a change in the manner in which the action of the play is presented to us. This change in key is felt more in some soliloquies than in others; Shakespeare differentiated his use of this dramatic device also.

In its widest sense the art of the soliloquy in Shakespeare extends to the asides and to the soliloquizing utterances which occur at many points in the plays, and which are on the border-line between the soliloquy proper and the dialogue complete with partner. In this study it has only been possible to draw attention occasionally to these important types of utterance, which may be regarded as an approximation or as a preliminary to the soliloquy. A closer look at the construction of the dialogue will often contribute to a better understanding of the monologues. When, for instance, a speech is becoming detached from the partner situation and tending towards the monologue, this is evidence of Shakespeare's close observation of the real-life process of communication between two people. On the one hand there are examples of complete and mutual understanding, but, on the other hand, of talking at cross purposes, of unintentional but also of intentional misunderstandings, of sudden digressions – all in all a multiplicity of possibilities which can only be hinted at here. Within this wide range of forms of communication, or of partial and malfunctioning communication, soliloquizing speeches occur time and again; the partner or opposite number is forgotten because the speaker gives himself up to memories, thoughts and fantasies, losing himself in reverie, even if only for a moment, before taking up the thread of conversation once more. Long before modern drama exploited such problems of communication Shakespeare created the most subtle effects, which often remind us of our own difficulties with our fellow beings and which, in a good performance, make a powerful impression, be it comic or tragic. When we read Shakespeare's soliloquies, or listen to them, it sometimes occurs to us that we too are somehow predisposed towards the soliloquy. This helps us towards an understanding of these great speeches.

Of course one must be careful not to classify all speeches which are not directed towards the partner as soliloquizing speeches. Especially in Shakespeare's early plays, for instance in the three parts of *Henry VI*, there are passages in which the need to provide the audience with epic material or explanation of narrative, seems to make the dialogue less relevant to those involved in it.[18] It is necessary to differentiate in order to decide whether a particular passage really does belong to the soliloquizing type.

This is true also of the aside. Between its use as an informative hint to the audience, which continues the existing stage convention, and its emergence as a short monologue in the course of which the speaker entirely forgets his surroundings, the aside in Shakespeare can fulfil a wide range of functions.[19] It is developed into a fine tool for indirect characterization, for dialogue operating simultaneously on several levels, for preparation and for parenthesis, but also for involuntary self-revelation. Often the same categories and viewpoints are applicable as to the soliloquies. Macbeth's important asides in the third scene of the play have provided an excellent example of this type of utterance, serving to unveil the character of the speaker and to lead up to the great soliloquies which are to come. The classification by some critics of these central statements of Macbeth's as soliloquies and not as asides, is not arbitrary.

In this conclusion, attention has been drawn to different aspects of the art of the soliloquy in Shakespeare, but in the complexity of the drama they constantly merge. In the studies of individual soliloquies we have tried to show that Shakespeare often achieves several different effects at the same time, and it is perhaps in this simultaneity and variety that their greatest mystery lies.

Notes

INTRODUCTION

1 M.L. Arnold, *The Soliloquies of Shakespeare* (New York, 1911); L.A. Skiffington, *The History of English Soliloquy. Aeschylus to Shakespeare* (London and New York, 1985).

2 See Skiffington, *Soliloquy*, chs II, III.

3 See W. Clemen, *English Tragedy Before Shakespeare. The Development of Dramatic Speech* (London, 1961; repr. 1980).

4 Matthew Arnold, 'Preface' to the first edition of *Poems* (1853), repr. in: Kenneth Allott, ed., *The Poems of Matthew Arnold* (London, 1965), 591.

5 Daniel Seltzer, 'The actors and staging', in *A New Companion to Shakespeare Studies*, ed. K. Muir and S. Schoenbaum (Cambridge, 1971), 47.

6 See M.C. Gingrich, *Soliloquies, Asides and Audience in English Renaissance Drama*, unpubl. Ph.D. Thesis (Rutgers University, New Brunswick, 1978), 7–8, and Robert Weimann, *Shakespeare and the Popular Tradition in the Theatre*, (Baltimore and London, 1978), 213–15.

7 J.R. Brown, 'On the acting of Shakespeare's plays' (1953), repr. in *The Seventeenth Century Stage*, ed. E. Bentley, (Chicago, 1968), 44.

8 This is the basis, for instance, of the definition found in J.T. Shipley's *Dictionary of World Literary Terms*, (London, 1970), 203: 'A Soliloquy is spoken by one person that is alone or acts as though he were alone. It is a kind of talking to oneself, not intended to affect others.'

9   John Barton, *Playing Shakespeare* (London and New York, 1984), 94.

10 F.L. Lucas, *Seneca and Elizabethan Tragedy* (Cambridge, 1922); C.W. Mendell, *Our Seneca* (Yale, 1941), ch V.

11 T.S. Eliot, 'Shakespeare and the stoicism of Seneca', *Selected Essays, 1917–1932* (London, 1932), 129.

12 See W. Roessler, *The Soliloquy in German Drama* (New York, 1915), 10.

13 *An Essay on Poetry* (London, 1717), 308.

14 *English Dramatists of Today* (London, 1882), 274.

15 M.C. Bradbrook, *Themes and Conventions of Elizabethan Tragedy* (London, 1935), esp. V, 'Conventions of speech'. In some reference works the influence of nineteenth century theories of drama may still be felt, as for instance in the entry on soliloquy in the *Encyclopaedia Britannica* (1977, 15th ed.): 'This device although somewhat artificial and therefore liable to ridicule, was long an accepted convention.'

16 A term used, amongst others, by Rudolf Stamm, *The Shaping Powers at Work* (Heidelberg, 1967), 32–51; he investigates passages which 'mirror' the action by indicating gestures, facial expression and stage business.

2   SOLILOQUIES FROM THE HISTORY PLAYS

1   See W. Clemen, 'Some aspects of style in the *Henry VI* plays', in *Shakespeare's Styles. Essays in Honour of Kenneth Muir*, ed. Ph. Edwards, I.-S. Ewbank, G.K. Hunter (Cambridge, 1980), 9–24.

2   A detailed discussion of these two soliloquies, which looks more closely at the historical perspective, may be found in W. Clemen, *A Commentary on Shakespeare's 'Richard III'* (London, 1968).

3   See Anne Righter, *Shakespeare and the Idea of the Play* (London, 1964), 95–100.

4   For a survey of stage business accompanying this soliloquy see Julie Hankey, ed., '*Richard III*'. *Plays in Performance* (London, 1981), 86–90. Anthony Sher's *Year of the King* (London, 1985), is a fascinating account of the actor creating his bottle-spidered hunchback for the RSC production of 1984.

5   For this soliloquy as expression of Shakespeare's heightened

understanding of tragedy, see K. Muir, 'Shakespeare's soliloquies', in *Occidente* 67 (1964), 48.

6 On conscience as one of the play's major themes see E.A.J. Honigmann (ed.), *King Richard the Third* (New Penguin Shakespeare, Harmondsworth, 1968), 22, 31; also R.B. Heilman, 'Satiety and conscience', in *Antioch Review* 24 (1964).

7 M.W. Merchant, *Shakespeare and the Artist* (London, 1959), 45; (see also its reproduction of Hogarth's painting, plate 6b).

8 Judith Cook, *Shakespeare's Players* (London, 1983), 43.

9 For this monologue see also Stanley Wells (ed.), *Richard II* (New Penguin Shakespeare, Harmondsworth, 1969), 35–7; R.D. Altick, 'Symphonic imagery in *Richard II*', in *PMLA* 62 (1947), 339–65; Winifred Nowottny, *The Language Poets Use* (London, 1962), 87–91; Derek Traversi, *An Approach to Shakespeare* (London, 1969), I, 173–5.

10 Helen Gardner sees in this thought-play undertaken for its own sake the chief difference from a metaphysical conceit; cf. *The Metaphysical Poets*, ed. H. Gardner (rev. ed. London, 1967), 19–20.

11 John Gielgud, *Stage Directions* (London, 1963), 30.

12 See W. Clemen, 'Shakespeare and Marlowe', in *Shakespeare 1971*, ed. C. Leech and J.M.R. Margeston (Toronto, 1972), 131; also Michael Manheim, *The Weak King Dilemma* (Syracuse, 1973), 65.

13 For a survey of criticism see J.C. Van de Water, 'The Bastard in *King John*', in *Shakespeare Quarterly* 11 (1960), 137–46.

14 See J.L. Calderwood, 'Commodity and honour in *King John*', in *University of Toronto Quarterly* 29 (1960), 341–56.

15 See W. Clemen, *English Tragedy Before Shakespeare. The Development of Dramatic Speech* (London, 1961; repr. 1980), 225–52.

16 For the crown as an 'attribute of royalty' in Shakespeare see M.H. Fleischer, *The Iconography of the English History Play* (Salzburg, 1974), 46, 65–97.

17 See T.F. Wharton, *'Henry the Fourth, Parts 1 & 2.' Text and Performance* (London, 1983), 45–53, for a comparison of this key theme in four widely different productions.

18   Sigmund Freud, *Jokes and their Relation to the Unconscious*, (Harmondsworth, 1976), 297.

19   See Robert Weimann, *Shakespeare and the Popular Tradition in the Theatre*, (Baltimore and London, 1978) especially 151–60.

20   Charles Barber calls him an 'anachronism' in a world dominated by 'base and rotten policy', *The Theme of Honour's Tongue. A Study of Social Attitudes in the English Drama from Shakespeare to Dryden* (Göteburg, 1985), 68.

3   SOLILOQUIES FROM THE COMEDIES AND ROMANCES

1   As Robert Weimann has shown, Launce moves between the real-life situation of a clown confronting a theatre audience, and the dramatic situation of a character within a world of the play. 'Laughing with the audience in *Two Gentlemen of Verona*: Shakespeare and the popular tradition of comedy', in *Shakespeare Survey* 22 (1969), 35–40.

2   See H.F. Brooks, 'Two clowns in a comedy (to say nothing of the dog): Speed, Launce (and Crab) in *The Two Gentlemen of Verona*', in *Essays and Studies* 16 (1963), 91–100.

3   See Brian Vickers, *The Artistry of Shakespeare's Prose* (London, 1968), 45.

4   Alexander Leggatt, *Shakespeare's Comedy of Love* (London, 1974), 22.

5   For a discussion of the reflexive mirror passages in this scene see Jörg Hasler, *Shakespeare's Theatrical Notation: The Comedies* (Bern, 1974), 124–7.

6   It was this aspect of the social climber, of the 'petty, ambitious vulgarian', that Laurence Olivier made memorable in the fifties; see J.R. Brown 'Directions for *Twelfth Night*' (1966), repr. in D.J. Palmer (ed.), *Shakespeare. 'Twelfth Night'. A Casebook* (London, 1972), 189.

7   As has been noted (Vickers, op. cit., 235), the style of this sequence of recommendations is modelled on the aphorisms of Gabriel Harvey's *Marginalia* and Bacon's *Essays*, those 'politic authors' (161) whose works Malvolio proposes to read in his new role as 'statesman'.

8   Historical surveys of interpretations of Malvolio on the stage can be found in J.M. Lothian and T.W. Craik (eds),

Twelfth Night, New Arden Shakespeare, London, 1975, xc–xciii, and in E. Story Donno (ed.), *Twelfth Night* (New Cambridge Shakespeare, Cambridge, 1985), 28–33. On Barton's 1969–72 production see Stanley Wells, 'Royal Shakespeare', in *Furman Studies* 23 (1976), 43–63.

9   On this aspect see C.L. Barber, *Shakespeare's Festive Comedies* (Princeton, 1959).

10 See D.N. Siegel, 'Malvolio: comic Puritan automaton', in M. Charney (ed.), *Shakespearean Comedy* (New York, 1980), 217–30.

11 Charles Lamb based his remarks on his impressions of the interpretation of the part by the late eighteenth-century actor Robert Bensley, who 'threw over the part an air of Spanish loftiness. He looked, spake, and moved like an old Castilian'. (D.J. Palmer, ed., *Casebook*, 40).

12 For a survey of critical comments on Helena see J.P. Price, *The unfortunate Comedy. A Study of 'All's Well That Ends Well' and its Critics* (Liverpool, 1968); J.L. Styan, *Shakespeare in Performance: 'All's Well That Ends Well'*, (Manchester, 1984), 16–20.

13 See further Nicholas Brooke, *'All's Well That Ends Well'*, *Shakespeare Survey* 30 (1977), 74.

14 For introductory material see Nigel Alexander, *Shakespeare: 'Measure for Measure'* (London, 1975), and the essays in C.K. Stead (ed.), *Shakespeare's 'Measure for Measure'. A Casebook* (London, 1971).

15 See D.J. McGinn, 'The precise Angelo', in *J.Q. Adams Memorial Studies*, ed. J.G. McManaway (Washington, 1948), 131.

16 As well as the implication of the fallen angel (cf. 'angel on the outward side', II.ii.265), Angelo's name involves a play of words on the coin 'angel'; Angelo is a false coin, not made of pure metal as he seemed to be.

17 On this passage see William Empson, 'Sense in *Measure for Measure*', in *The Structure of Complex Words* (London, 1951), 276.

18 Ernest Schanzer, *The Problem Plays of Shakespeare* (London, 1963), 93.

19 On this matter see Barbara Mowat, *The Dramaturgy of Shakespeare's Romances* (Athens Ga., 1976), 35–94.

20 Imogen's soliloquy IV.ii.291–332 is the only comparable one with regard to complexity of dramatic effect and language.

21 In the poem *The Rape of Lucrece* written in the 1590s Shakespeare had already treated this material, in narrative form.

22 H. Granville-Barker, *Prefaces to Shakespeare*, first publ. 1930 (London, 1958), I, 512.

23 This was already emphasized by S.T. Coleridge: 'Everybody will call to mind the grandeur of the language of Prospero in that divine speech, where he takes leave of his magic art', T. Hawkes (ed.), *Coleridge on Shakespeare* (Penguin Shakespeare Library, Harmondsworth, 1969), 238.

24 Thus Anne Righter feels the play to be 'deliberately enigmatic' and 'an extraordinarily secretive work of art'; Introduction to *The Tempest* (New Penguin Shakespeare, Harmondsworth, 1968), 12.

25 Hawkes (ed.), *Coleridge*, 224.

26 C.J. Sisson, 'The magic of Prospero', *Shakespeare Survey* 11 (1958), 70–7.

27 On the transitions and the dramatic rhythms of this passage see J.R. Brown, *Shakespeare: The Tempest* (London, 1969), 56.

28 From the abundant literature on this question, which has been answered in many different ways, see the following: W.C. Curry, *Shakespeare's Philosophical Patterns* (Baton Rouge, 1937), 163–99; Frank Kermode (ed.), *The Tempest* (New Arden Shakespeare, London, 1958), xlvii–li; R.H. West, 'Ceremonial magic in *The Tempest*', in *Shakespearean Essays*, ed A. Thaler and N. Sanders (Knoxville, 1964), 63–78; D.G. James, *The Dream of Prospero* (Oxford, 1967), 45–71; D.W. Pearson, '"Unless I be reliev'd by prayer": *The Tempest* in perspective' *Shakespeare Studies* 7 (1974), 253–82.

29 J.P. Cutts, 'Music and the supernatural in *The Tempest*' (1958), repr. in D.J. Palmer (ed.), *Shakespeare. 'The Tempest'. A Casebook* (London, 1968), 206.

30 On the theme of forgiveness and reconciliation see R.G. Hunter, *Shakespeare and the Comedy of Forgiveness* (New York, 1965), 227–41.

31 See Bonamy Dobrée, '*The Tempest*', *Essays and Studies* 5 (1952), 13–25; esp. 23–5.

32 Frank Kermode, *Shakespeare: The Final Plays* (London, 1963), 49.

4   SOLILOQUIES FROM THE TRAGEDIES

1   J.R. Brown, *Shakespeare's Dramatic Style* (London, 1970), 44–52, offers a detailed analysis of this soliloquy (and the dialogue that follows it), taking into account the implied action on the stage as well as the nuances of versification and vocabulary.

2   On the function of the garden wall, and on the treatment of time, see Emrys Jones, *Scenic Form in Shakespeare* (Oxford, 1971), 34–6. Details of problems and traditions of staging the play are given in G.B. Evans (ed.), *Romeo and Juliet*, New Cambridge Shakespeare, Cambridge, 1984, 28–48.

3   On the imagery here and in the other soliloquies, see W. Clemen, *The Development of Shakespeare's Imagery* (London, 2nd ed. 1977), 67–73. Michael Goldman refers to the use of the stage, underlining 'the strain that the effort toward contact demands of them – in Romeo's yearning upward toward the balcony, the perilous rope-ladder descent, the crowbars and torches breaking into the tomb.' (*Shakespeare and the Energies of Drama*, Princeton, 1972, 40.)

4   See Caroline Spurgeon, *Shakespeare's Imagery and what it Tells us* (Cambridge, 1935), 310–16.

5   On Shakespeare's skill in this and in the other soliloquies under discussion, 'in suiting changes of style to changes of mood', see Harry Levin, 'Form and formality in *Romeo and Juliet*', *Shakespeare Quarterly* 11 (1960), 3–11; also the detailed interpretation in Brian Gibbons (ed.), *Romeo and Juliet* (New Arden Shakespeare, London, 1980), 57–60, and in L.A. Skiffington, *The History of English Soliloquy. Aeschylus to Shakespeare* (London and New York, 1985), 105–7.

6   'Her words emerge from a triple layer of ignorance', writes Bertrand Evans, *Shakespeare's Tragic Practice* (Oxford, 1979), 34.

7   G.M. McCown reaches this conclusion in his essay '"Run-nawayes eyes" and Juliet's epithalamium', *Shakespeare Quarterly* 28 (1976), 150–70, which looks closely at the

literary tradition of the epithalamium and Shakespeare's departures from the conventions.

8   See H. Granville-Barker, *Prefaces*, II, 347: 'To the modern Juliet . . . this scene probably presents more difficulties than any other in the play. Victorian Juliets customarily had theirs drastically eased by the eliminating of "Gallop apace . . ." on the grounds – God save the mark! – of its immodesty. One hopes that the last has been heard of such nonsense.'

9   On 'the absorption of the sonnet mode into the art of the play' here and in other scenes see Gibbons (ed.), *Romeo and Juliet*, 43–52.

10 Juliet's maturing into womanhood is discussed by I.G. Dash, *Wooing, Wedding and Power: Women in Shakespeare's Plays* (New York, 1981), 67–100.

11 See G.K. Hunter, 'Shakespeare's earliest tragedies: *Titus Andronicus* and *Romeo and Juliet*', *Shakespeare Survey* 27 (1974), 8.

12 See II.ii.3; II.ii.19 ff; III.ii.19; III.ii.22.

13 For the stage business, the indirect stage directions and for the vocabulary of this soliloquy see Brown, *Dramatic Style*, 57–63.

14 See Nevill Coghill, *Shakespeare's Professional Skills* (Cambridge, 1964), 142 ff.

15 On the significance of the nocturnal setting see Jones, *Scenic Form*, 47. A survey of the play's stage history may be found in John Ripley's *'Julius Caesar' on Stage in England and America, 1599–1973* (Cambridge, 1980).

16 A selection of contradictory assessments of Brutus is presented in Peter Ure (ed.), *'Julius Caesar'. A Casebook* (London, 1969).

17 S.T. Coleridge, 'Marginalia on *Julius Caesar*' (1808), in Ure (ed.), *Casebook*, 32.

18 J.D. Wilson throws light on this first sentence in the introduction to his edition of *Julius Caesar* (Cambridge, 1949), xxx–xxxi, aptly summarized by T.S. Dorsch (ed.), *Julius Caesar* (New Arden Shakespeare, London, 1955, 33).

19 See for instance the remarks in Ure (ed.), *Casebook*, by Edward Dowden, 34; J.I.M. Stewart, 115–16; L.C.

Knights, 128–33; V.K. Whitaker, 174–8; E. Schanzer, 186–92; Mark Hunter, 201–2.

20 Some critics, however, defend Brutus's position, and feel his fear of the tyrant to be that of a radical republican, meriting serious consideration; see for instance Robert Ornstein, 'Seneca and the political drama of *Julius Caesar*', in *Journal of English and Germanic Philology* 57 (1958), 51–6, or A.D. Nuttall, *A New Mimesis. Shakespeare and the Representation of Reality* (London, 1983), 107–9.

21 See above all Schanzer, *Problem Plays*, 10–70, and E.A.J. Honigmann, *Shakespeare: Seven Tragedies. The Dramatist's Manipulation of Response* (London, 1976), 30–53.

22 For elucidation of this difficult passage see Dorsch (ed.), *Julius Caesar*, 37.

23 See R.A. Brewer, *Hero & Saint. Shakespeare and the Graeco-Roman Tradition* (Oxford, 1971), 226: 'The effect of this brief soliloquy . . . is to impart to the drama of Brutus a tragic tenderness'.

24 Thus H. Granville-Barker says of the suprapersonal quality of this soliloquy: 'This is a recipe for tragedy. Brutus is speaking but it might well be Macbeth'. *From 'Henry V' to 'Hamlet'*, British Academy Annual Shakespeare Lecture (London, 1925), 17.

25 On the use of personification at this point see David Daiches, *Shakespeare's 'Julius Caesar'* (London, 1976), 24.

26 I.ii.129 ff; I.v.92 ff; II.ii.543 ff; III.i.56 ff; III.ii.379 ff; III.iii.73 ff; IV.iv.32 ff. On Hamlet's soliloquies see especially Harold Jenkins (ed.), *Hamlet* (The New Arden Shakespeare, London, 1981), to whose observations this chapter owes a great deal; the notes on the passages under discussion should also be consulted. There are valuable contributions in John Jump (ed.), *'Hamlet'. A Casebook* (London, 1968), and in David Bevington (ed.), *Twentieth Century Interpretations of 'Hamlet'*, (Englewood Cliffs, N.J., 1968). A summary of earlier interpretations is given in L. Schücking, *The Meaning of 'Hamlet'* (Oxford, 1937). There are detailed discussions of the soliloquies in Harry Levin, *The Question of 'Hamlet'* (New York, 1959); in Nigel Alexander, *Poison, Play, and Duel. A Study in 'Hamlet'*

(London, 1971), especially ch III; and in L.S. Champion, '"By indirections find directions out". The soliloquies in *Hamlet*', in *The Journal of General Education* 27 (1976), 265–80.

27 See R.A. Foakes, 'Character and speech in *Hamlet*', in J.R. Brown and B. Harris (eds), *Hamlet*, Stratford-upon-Avon Studies 5 (London, 1963), 148–62, and I.-S. Ewbank, '*Hamlet* and the power of words', *Shakespeare Survey* 30 (1977), 85–102.

28 Thus Anne Barton: 'His four major soliloquies after encountering the ghost . . . are much more evasive . . . than the equivalent speeches of an Othello or a Macbeth', Introduction to *Hamlet*, New Penguin Shakespeare (Harmondsworth, 1980), 40.

29 See Robert Hapgood, 'Hamlet nearly absurd: the dramaturgy of delay', *Tulane Drama Review* 9 (1965), 132–45, and, from a rather different point of view, John Holloway, in Jump (ed.), *Casebook*, 163. For a divergent view of the hesitation and delay see Philip Brockbank, 'Hamlet the bonesetter', *Shakespeare Survey* 30 (1977), 109.

30 For implied stage-directions, including details of stress and intonation, see Peter Davison, '*Hamlet*'. *Text and Performance* (London, 1983). There are informative illustrations in H. Marshall, (ed. and introd.), '*Hamlet*' *through the Ages. A Pictorial Record from 1709*, compiled by Raymond Mander and Joe Mitchenson (London, 1952); also in W.A. Buell, *The Hamlets of the Theatre* (New York, 1968). On recent productions see Richard David, *Shakespeare in the Theatre* (Cambridge, 1978).

31 See Barton, Introduction to *Hamlet*, 40.

32 'Interruptiveness is a dominant characteristic of Hamlet's soliloquies', J.L. Calderwood, *To Be and Not to Be. Negation and Metadrama in 'Hamlet'* (New York, 1983), 156.

33 On Hamlet's tendency to generalize, see Levin, *Question of 'Hamlet'*, 60. Theodore Spencer sees it as 'one of the most important and attractive sides of Hamlet's character', *Shakespeare and the Nature of Man*, (New York, 1942, 2nd ed. 1961) 100.

34 And yet, 'Rehabilitation-passages generally follow after he

has been shown at his worst', as is shown by Honigmann, *Tragedies*, 67. For the audience's changing response to Hamlet see also R.W. Desai, 'Hamlet's soliloquies and Shakespeare's audience', *Hamlet Studies* 5 (1983), 66–74.

35 W. Clemen, 'Appearance and reality in Shakespeare's plays', in *Shakespeare's Dramatic Art. Collected Essays* (London, 1972), 163–88.

36 A psychoanalytical interpretation of this soliloquy may be found in Theodore Lidz, *Hamlet's Enemy: Madness and Myth in 'Hamlet'* (London, 1976), 49–54.

37 On 'sullied' see the detailed longer note in Jenkins (ed.), *Hamlet*, 436.

38 See Granville-Barker, *Prefaces*, I, 5 ff.

39 Jenkins rightly comments: 'Already, before *his* task has come to him, Hamlet gives an indication of his feeling of inadequacy' (see New Arden, note on I.ii.153).

40 Jenkins (ed.), *Hamlet*, 484–93, provides a survey of the most important interpretations, as well as illuminating and detailed explanations, which are well beyond the scope of our discussion. Further surveys of scholarly opinion may be found in I.T. Richards, 'The meaning of Hamlet's soliloquy', *PMLA* 48 (1933), 741–4; also in A. Newell, 'The dramatic context and meaning of Hamlet's "To be or not to be" soliloquy', *PMLA* 80 (1965), 38–50, and Vincent Petronella, 'Hamlet "To be or not to be" soliloquy: Once more unto the breach', *Studies in Philology* 71 (1974), 72–88. See also G.R. Elliott, *Scourge and Minister: A Study of 'Hamlet' as a Tragedy of Revengefulness and Justice* (1951, repr. New York, 1965), 73–7, and R.M. Frye, *The Renaissance 'Hamlet'. Issues and Responses in 1600* (Princeton, NJ, 1984), 188–93.
    The stimulating New Cambridge edition of *Hamlet* by Philip Edward (Cambridge, 1985) came to the author's attention only after completion of this book. Edwards argues, in contrast to Jenkins, that suicide is the central issue of this soliloquy, the 'plain truth' of which he considers to be 'that death is better than life but that we haven't got the courage to kill ourselves' (27; see also 47–50).

41 See J. Dover Wilson, *What Happens in 'Hamlet'* (Cambridge, 1935), 127 ff.

42 'Notes on the plays: *Hamlet*', in John Wain (ed.), *Johnson as Critic* (London, 1973), 242.

43 J.W. Draper offers a precise analysis of the changing tempo in *The Tempo-Patterns of Shakespeare's Plays* (Heidelberg, 1957), 85–6; on this aspect see also J.R. Brown, 'The setting for *Hamlet*', in Brown and Harris (eds), *Hamlet*, 163–84, especially 179–83.

44 Details may be found in the chapter 'Interrogation' in Levin, *Question of 'Hamlet'*, 17–43. See also Maynard Mack, 'The world of *Hamlet*' (1952), repr. in Jump (ed.), *Casebook*, 88: 'Hamlet's world is pre-eminently in the interrogative mood'; and Robert Hapgood, '*Hamlet* and its thematic modes of speech', in W.G. Holzberger and P.B. Waldeck (eds), *Perspectives on 'Hamlet'* (Lewisburg, 1975), 29–47.

45 On this feature of style see Maurice Charney, *Style in 'Hamlet'* (Princeton, NJ, 1969), 301–2.

46 See the detailed analysis of the soliloquy in Bertram Joseph, *Conscience and the King. A study of 'Hamlet'* (London, 1953), 112.

47 On the futility and the repeatedly negative answers to the questions posed in this soliloquy see, among others, L.C. Knights, *An Approach to 'Hamlet'* (London, 1961), 79.

48 On 'shuffled off' see J.T.B. Spencer's explanatory note in the New Penguin edition, 268: 'like a snake shedding its slough, or perhaps a butterfly – a symbol of the soul – emerging from its chrysalis'. On the other hand, in the New Arden edition, 279, Jenkins says of 'coil': 'It includes all the appurtenances, occupations and experiences of mortal life'.

49 See Spurgeon, *Imagery*, 316–19, and Clemen, *Imagery*, 111–18.

50 There is a detailed commentary on the soliloquies discussed in this chapter in Kenneth Muir (ed.), *Macbeth* (New Arden Shakespeare, London, 1951), l–lxxiv, and G.R. Elliott, *Dramatic Providence in 'Macbeth'* (Princeton, 1980), 52–75.

51 On the use made of the letter see also K.E. Moroney, *The Letter as a Dramatic Device in Shakespeare's Plays*, unpubl. Ph.D. Thesis (Norman, Oklahoma, 1956).

52 Marvin Rosenberg, *The Masks of 'Macbeth'* (Berkeley, 1978), especially 158–242, shows the wide range of first

impressions of Lady Macbeth as conveyed by different actresses in his comprehensive documentation of the play's stage history. See also G. Lloyd Evans, '*Macbeth:* 1946–80 at Stratford-upon-Avon', in J.R. Brown (ed.), *Focus on 'Macbeth'* (London, 1982), 87–110.

53   See John Bayley, *Shakespeare and Tragedy* (London, 1981), 186.

54   The sequence of words 'do . . . do . . . undone' will be picked up again in Macbeth's first soliloquy (I.vii.1 ff).

55   Compare the words with which Iago describes his intended poisoning of Othello: 'I'll pour this pestilence into his ear' (*Othello* II.iii.347); also the dumbshow in *Hamlet*.

56   On the symbols in Macbeth see Spurgeon, *Imagery*, 329 ff, and Kenneth Muir, 'Image and symbol in *Macbeth*', in *Shakespeare the Professional* (London, 1973), 128–57.

57   Further details may be found in W.M. Merchant, '"His Fiend-like Queen"', *Shakespeare Survey* 19 (1966), 75–81. Echoes of Medea are traced in I.-S. Ewbank, '"The Fiend-like Queen". A note on *Macbeth* and Seneca's *Medea*', *Shakespeare Survey* 19 (1966), 82–94.

58   See J.R. Brown, *Shakespeare: 'The Tragedy of Macbeth'* (London, 1963), 32.

59   A detailed discussion of this soliloquy, which draws attention to individual points not dwelt on here, may be found in John Baxter, *Shakespeare's Poetic Style* (London, 1980), 207–14; this includes comments on the interpretations of F.R. Leavis, and of Yvor Winters (on the dagger soliloquy).

60   On 'done' see M.M. Mahood, *Shakespeare's Wordplay* (London, 1957), 136–8.

61   See Clemen, *Imagery*, 98.

62   Divergent comments on this difficult passage are collected in Terence Hawkes (ed.), *Twentieth Century Interpretations of 'Macbeth'* (Englewood Cliffs, N.J., 1977); compare especially Cleanth Brooks, 'The naked babe and the cloak of manliness' (1947), 34–53, and the replies of O.J. Campbell, 'Shakespeare and the new critics' (1948), 54–9 and Helen Gardner, 'A reply to Cleanth Brooks' (1959), 76–82.

63   On the subject of regicide see Maynard Mack, Jr., *Killing the King* (New Haven, Conn., 1973), 190–1.

64 On the problems that this scene poses for the actor see Peter Hall in an interview with J.R. Brown: 'The audience only see a dagger if he sees a dagger. . . . Theatricality, in the proper sense, is part of Shakespeare's drama and I could make a case that the incident of the airborne dagger is the actor Macbeth getting his props ready . . .' ('Directing Shakespeare', in Brown (ed.), *Focus*, 237).

65 On evil in this play as an all-pervading perversion of the natural state in the individual, the body politic and the universe see G.W. Knight, *The Imperial Theme* (London, 1931), 125–35. There is a detailed discussion of the same theme in P.A. Jorgensen, *Our Naked Frailties. Sensational Art and Meaning in 'Macbeth'* (Berkeley, 1971), 41–58.

66 For a survey of the stage history and the divergent critics' views see Marvin Rosenberg, *The Masks of 'Othello'* (Berkeley, 1961). A valuable collection of actors' criticism of *Othello* is to be found in C.J. Carlisle, *Shakespeare from the Greenroom* (Chapel Hill, 1969), 172–263.

67 See R.B. Heilman, *Magic in the Web, Action and Language in 'Othello'* (Lexington, 1956), 152.

68 See Barton, *Playing Shakespeare* (London and New York, 1984), 99.

69 It had also occurred to Othello to poison Desdemona, but Iago had advised him against it and recommended another form of death: 'Do it not with poison, strangle her in her bed, even the bed she hath contaminated' (IV.i.203–4).

70 On the disintegration of Othello's world of rhetorical order see Giorgio Melchiori, 'The rhetoric of character construction: *Othello*', *Shakespeare Survey* 34 (1981), 61–72.

71 Earlier critics assumed that Othello would enter at this point as the noble Moor, restored to all his former dignity; see A.C. Bradley, *Shakespearean Tragedy* (first publ. 1904; London and New York, 1960), 175–206 and Spencer, *Nature of Man*, 130.

72 See R.F. Wilson, Jr., 'Symbol and character: the function of Othello's candle (V.ii.1–22)', in *Literatur in Wissenschaft und Unterricht* 14 (1981), 29–35.

73 In Verdi's opera *Otello* the same melody is heard at this moment as during the kiss at the end of the first act. See

Winton Dean, 'Verdi's *Otello*: a Shakespearian master-piece', in *Shakespeare Survey* 21 (1968), 92.

74 Thorough interpretations of the text are given in John Money, 'Othello's "It is the cause . . .": an analysis', in *Shakespeare Survey* 6 (1953), 94–105; and in Jane Adamson, '*Othello' as Tragedy: Some Problems of Judgement and Feeling* (Cambridge, 1980), 264–71.

75 On changing attitudes towards Othello see Helen Gardner, '*Othello*. A retrospect, 1900–67', *Shakespeare Survey* 21 (1968), 1–12.

76 'Cause' seems to be used as a legal term here. The sentence might be paraphrased: 'It is the judicial procedure with respect to adultery which drives me to do this, to kill Desdemona'; see W.C. Foreman, Jr., *The Music of the Close. The Final Scenes of Shakespeare's Tragedies* (Lexington, 1978), 164; see also 163–6 for a discussion of Othello's perversion of justice.

77 See E.A.J. Honigmann, 'Shakespeare's "bombast"', in *Shakespeare's Styles. Essays in Honour of Kenneth Muir*, 159; as also L.C. Knights, 'Rhetoric and insincerity', ibid., 7.

78 G.W. Knight, 'The *Othello* music', in *The Wheel of Fire* (rev. ed., London, 1949), 104.

79 On the varieties of obscurity in the play see S.P. Zitner, '*King Lear* and its language', in R.L. Colie and F.T. Flahiffs (eds), *Some Facets of 'King Lear'. Essays in Prismatic Criticism* (London, 1974), 3–22.

80 A thorough description of Lear's speech is given in Winifred Nowottny, 'Some aspects of the style of *King Lear*', in *Shakespeare Survey* 13 (1960), 49–57.

81 Michael Goldman examines the histrionic imagery in this and in other scenes in the play, '*King Lear*: acting and feeling', in Lawrence Danson (ed.), *On 'King Lear'* (Princeton, N.J., 1981), 25–46.

82 This is demonstrated in R.B. Heilman, *This Great Stage. Image and Structure in 'King Lear'*, Baton Rouge, 1948; compare also Kenneth Muir, *Shakespeare 'King Lear'. A Critical Study* (Penguin Masterstudies, Harmondsworth, 1986), 36–51.

83 G.K. Hunter (ed.), *King Lear* (New Penguin Shakespeare, Harmondsworth, 1972), 44.

84   Maynard Mack, *'King Lear' in Our Time* (London, 1965), 110–11, comments on this.

5   CONCLUSION

1   For examples of these conventions see M.L. Arnold, *The Soliloquies of Shakespeare* (New York, 1911), 47–72.

2   Thus in *King Lear*, for example, the soliloquy of Kent (II.ii.160–73), or that of Edgar (II.iii).

3   See J.L. Styan, *Shakespeare's Stagecraft* (Cambridge, 1967), 72–5, 163–71.

4   On the preparation and positioning of the soliloquy in the action see Nevill Coghill, *Shakespeare's Professional Skills* (Cambridge, 1964), 142–53.

5   See S.S. Hussey, 'The development of the soliloquy', in *The Literary Language of Shakespeare* (London, 1982), 181–202.

6   On this point see Robert Weimann, *Shakespeare and the Popular Tradition in the Theatre* (Baltimore and London, 1978), 253–60.

7   See Rudolf Stamm, 'The theatrical physiognomy of Shakespeare's plays', in *The Shaping Powers at Work* (Heidelberg, 1967), 11–84; W.D. Smith, *Shakespeare's Playhouse Practice* (Hanover, 1975), 13–22; A.P. Slater, *Shakespeare the Director* (Brighton, 1982).

8   See W. Clemen, *English Tragedy Before Shakespeare. The Development of Dramatic Speech* (London, 1961; repr. 1980), 44–55.

9   Una Ellis-Fermor has described this skilful adumbration as 'a technique that indicates character by touches, by silences, by omissions', (*Shakespeare the Dramatist*, ed. K. Muir, London, 1961, 30).

10   See Anne Barton, 'Shakespeare and the limits of language', in *Shakespeare Survey* 24 (1971), 19–30; I.-S. Ewbank, '"More pregnantly than words": some uses and limitations of visual symbolism', in *Shakespeare Survey* 24 (1971), 13–18.

11   See Slater, *Shakespeare The Director*, 121–36.

12   See W. Clemen, 'Past and future in Shakespeare's drama', *Proceedings of the British Academy* 52 (1967), 231–52.

13   On this point see the three studies by L.S. Champion: *The Evolution of Shakespeare's Comedy. A Study in Dramatic Perspect-*

ive (Cambridge, Mass., 1967); *Shakespeare's Tragic Perspective* (Athens, Ga., 1976); *Perspectives in Shakespeare's English Histories* (Athens, Ga., 1980).

14 See Honigmann, 'Response and dramatic perspective', in *Shakespeare: Seven Tragedies. The Dramatist's Manipulation of Response* (London, 1976), 16–29.

15 This 'discrepant awareness' has been discussed by Bertram Evans, *Shakespeare's Comedies* (Oxford, 1960), and *Shakespeare's Tragic Practice* (Oxford, 1979).

16 See for instance L.L. Schücking, *Character Problems in Shakespeare's Plays* (1922; repr. Gloucester, Mass., 1959), 29–52.

17 Ellis-Fermor, *Shakespeare. The Dramatist*, 14.

18 See W. Clemen, 'Some aspects of style in the *Henry VI* plays', in *Shakespeare's Styles. Essays in Honour of Kenneth Muir*, ed. Ph. Edwards, I.-S. Ewbank, G.K. Hunter (Cambridge, 1980), 9–24.

19 See S.L. Bethell, *Shakespeare and the Popular Tradition* (London, 1944), 87–90; A.C. Sprague, *Shakespeare and the Audience* (Cambridge, Mass., 1935), 59–96; J.L. Styan, 'The actor at the foot of Shakespeare's platform', *Shakespeare Survey* 12 (1959), 56–63.

Select bibliography

This list only includes criticism dealing with Shakespeare's soliloquies in general; studies of individual soliloquies and related aspects are referred to in the notes. (In addition, as this book is designed for a predominantly English-speaking audience, the list omits the extensive references to German publications that were included in the original German version.)

Arnold, Morris Leroy, *The Soliloquies of Shakespeare. A Study in Technic* (New York, 1911).

Carson, Neil, 'The Elizabethan soliloquy – direct address or monologue?', in *Theatre Notebook* 30 (1976), 12–18.

Clemen, Wolfgang, *Shakespeare's Soliloquies*, The Presidential Address of the Modern Humanities Research Association, (Cambridge, 1964). Repr. in W. Clemen, *Shakespeare's Dramatic Art. Collected Essays* (London, 1972, repr. 1980), 147–62.

Shakespeares Monologe. Ein Zugang zu seiner dramatischen Kunst (München und Zürich, 1985).

Coghill, Nevill, 'Soliloquy', in *Shakespeare's Professional Skills*, (Cambridge, 1964), 128–63.

Ellis-Fermor, Una, 'A technical problem: the revelation of unspoken thought in drama', in *The Frontiers of Drama* (London, 1945, 2nd ed. 1964), 96–126.

'Communication in thought', in *Shakespeare the Dramatist and other papers*, ed. Kenneth Muir (London, 1961), 102–24.

Gingrich, Margaret Coleman, *Soliloquies, Asides, and Audience in English Renaissance Drama*, unpubl. Ph.D. Thesis (Rutgers University, New Brunswick, 1978).

Hussey, S.S., 'The development of the soliloquy', in *The Literary Language of Shakespeare* (London and New York, 1982), 181–202.

Muir, Kenneth, 'Shakespeare's soliloquies', in *Occidente* 67 (1964), 45–58.

Rappaport, Gideon, *Some Special Uses of the Soliloquy in Shakespeare*, unpubl. Ph.D. Thesis (Brandeis University, 1979).

Skiffington, Lloyd A., *The History of English Soliloquy. Aeschylus to Shakespeare* (London and New York, 1985).

Sprague, Arthur Colby, 'Some conventions', in *Shakespeare and the Audience. A Study in the Technique of Exposition* (Harvard, 1935, Repr. New York, 1966).

The Soliloquy extracts are taken from the following Arden editions:

King Richard III, ed. Antony Hammond (London, 1981).

King Richard II, ed. Peter Ure (London, 1961).

King John, ed. E.A.J. Honigmann (London, 1954).

The First Part of King Henry IV, ed. A.R. Humphreys (London, 1960).

The Second Part of King Henry IV, ed. A.R. Humphreys (London, 1966).

Twelfth Night, ed. J.M. Lothian and T.W. Craik (London, 1975).

The Two Gentlemen of Verona, ed. Clifford Leech (London, 1969).

All's Well That Ends Well, ed. G.K. Hunter (London, 1959).

Measure for Measure, ed. J.W. Lever (London, 1965).

Cymbeline, ed. J.M. Nosworthy (London, 1955).

The Tempest, ed. Frank Kermode (London, 1958).

Romeo and Juliet, ed. Brian Gibbons (London, 1980).

Julius Caesar, ed. T.S. Dorsch (London, 1955).

Hamlet, ed. Harold Jenkins (London, 1982).

Macbeth, ed. Kenneth Muir (London, 1962).

Othello, ed. M.R. Ridley (London, 1958).

King Lear, ed. Kenneth Muir (London, 1972).

Often the best-known and most memorable passages in Shakespeare's plays, the soliloquies also tend to be focal points in the drama. In this study of soliloquies from throughout Shakespeare's *oeuvre*, Professor Clemen provides us with insights not only into the characters' motives and thoughts, but also into Shakespeare's manipulation of audience response, the evocative power of his poetry and his skill in creating dramatic illusion.

Twenty-seven soliloquies are examined, not as isolated examples, but as intrinsic parts of the plays. Professor Clemen explains the context of each, showing how the spectator or reader is led to the soliloquy and how the drama is continued afterwards. He discusses the detailed structure of each soliloquy, while looking at it in terms of the surrounding drama, so that for those plays, such as *Romeo and Juliet*, *Hamlet* and *Macbeth*, from which several soliloquies are considered, the passages discussed serve as a basic structure for an interpretation of the whole play.

Professor Clemen is a distinguished Shakespeare scholar, and has lectured in various parts of Germany, Britain and the United States. He is currently Head of the Shakespeare Library at the University of Munich.

Also from Methuen

The Development of Shakespeare's Imagery
Wolfgang Clemen

Shakespeare's Wordplay
M. M. Mahood

Shakespeare
The poet in his world
M. C. Bradbrook

Cover illustration: Bob Peck as Macbeth.
Photograph: Donald Cooper.

Cover design: Juan Hayward

University Paperbacks
are published by

Methuen & Co. Ltd
11 New Fetter Lane
London EC4P 4EE

Methuen, Inc.
29 West 35th Street

ISBN 0-416-30460-5

9 780416 304602